IMPRESSIONS OF A WARTIME CHILDHOOD

IMPRESSIONS OF A WARTIME CHILDHOOD

JANET GALLON

Copyright © 2019 Janet Gallon

Published in Scotland by Anatta Books 2019

10 9 8 7 6 5 4 3 2 1

British Library Cataloguing in Publication Data. A catalogue record for this book is available from the British Library.

ISBN 978-0-9933344-3-6

Typeset in Garamond and Gill Sans (two popular typefaces of the WWII era)

For Sarah & Helen

CONTENTS

FOREWORD

From my own point of view, my childhood was wholly unremarkable. It was happy, ordinary and, quite definitely, nothing to write a book about.

From my children's point of view, my childhood was remarkable enough to be a constant source of wonderment. In their eyes, I was brought up in another era and almost in another world. They cannot go back in time to see that world for themselves. They can only ask endless questions about it and hope to find me in an expansive mood, with enough spare time to do justice to their curiosity.

The main difference between my childhood and theirs is that, whereas I was brought up in a city suburb, in the shadow of war and its attendant austerity, my children have lived all their lives in villages in the Scottish Highlands, in times of peace and plenty.

Because of this contrast in our backgrounds, I can understand why they ply me with questions about the days "when I was young". I am always pleased to answer because I realise that, mainly from watching old films on television, they have picked up some very odd – and wildly inaccurate – ideas about what life was like at home, in Britain, during the war. My elder daughter, for instance, had gained the impression that civilians spent all their time in air raid shelters, because of a perpetual blitz!

When it was suggested that I should write down my impressions of what it was like to grow up in the 1940's, I dismissed the notion, with the typical mother's protest that I had too many other things to do. But my children were so delighted with the idea that, to please them, I have made the time to put pen to paper. What I have recorded are the impressions that linger after thirty years or so. Sometimes they are vivid; sometimes they are vague. I kept no diaries and my memory has been my only guide. If, on any point of detail, it has let me down, I crave indulgence.

I. THE DAY WAR BROKE OUT

The spirit of my grandmother lingered in our house, although she had died the previous year, in 1938. Sundays continued to be observed in the old manner, no work being done on the Sabbath if it could be put off until Monday. Quietness was the order of the day, our family pastimes being nothing noisier than listening to selected radio programmes or reading a book – a good book, of course. Comics and other such "rubbish" were relegated to week-days. Grandma had taught us that, should we be so wicked as to knit or sew on a Sunday, our fingers would drop off and, although my sister and I dared to take this dogma with a pinch of salt, neither of us was willing to be the first to put it to the test. So it came about that I was quietly reading on the morning of Sunday, September 3rd 1939. I was reading, not a good book, but a Sunday newspaper. Very daring! Moreover, I was following the adventures of the famous cartoon-strip stars Tillie the Toiler and Wee Mac! Slowly but surely, Grandma's shade was losing her grip!

On those Sunday mornings when we did not go to church, it was my parents' habit to listen to the religious service on the wireless. It did not strike me as unusual therefore, when my father rose from his armchair by the fire about eleven o'clock and plugged in the wireless at the wall socket. I paid no special attention until I realised that what we were hearing was not the usual religious broadcast. A solemn voice, heavy with portent, was announcing, "This is London". I put down my newspaper. The Prime Minister, Mr Neville Chamberlain, began to speak and something in his tone compelled me to listen. He sounded tired and old, and very, very sad. I heard him say, "This country is at war with Germany", but I did not understand. I was only ten years old and what could I know of war?

Later, I wondered if the BBC had broadcast another programme after Mr Chamberlain's speech and if anyone, anywhere in Britain, had bothered to listen. Certainly in our house the wireless was switched off as soon as the fateful message had been delivered. My mother had come into the living-room from the kitchen, where she had been preparing lunch. She sat down opposite my father, tears on her cheeks. I had seen my mother cry only once before and that had been when Grandma died. Nobody spoke for what seemed like a long time.

With hindsight, I can imagine my parents' thoughts during those minutes of stunned silence. They, who were born in the 1880's, had already lived through two wars – the Boer War and the Great War, called sometimes "The war to end all wars". But here they were again. Where would it all end?

Sunday or not, action was called for. There was work to be done. Top priority had to be given to blacking out the windows, and my sister, three years my senior, was allowed to help in that task. Roller blinds were still in fashion, and unlike those of most of our neigh-bours, who favoured ecru linen trimmed with lace, ours were practical dark blue. That was a start and somehow, with thick brown paper and drawing pins, Mother contrived to close the gaps at the sides of the blinds so that we could have light in the house when darkness brought a black night to obliterate that black day. I felt quite out of things, surrounded as I was by most un-Sunday-like activity. The reason for it eluded me and no-one seemed to have time to answer my questions. I think I must have been a thorough nuisance.

We lived in a mid-terrace house in Kings Park, a Southside suburb of Glasgow, where people tended to keep themselves to themselves. My father worked in the headquarters of a major steel firm in the city. The neighbours in the other three houses that, with ours, made up the terrace, had similar white-collar, middle class jobs. We had lived in close proximity to each other for ten years, yet our lives had scarcely touched – until the war drew us all together. Privacy forgotten, that Sunday little knots of neighbours were to be seen all down our road, talking quietly over garden fences, comparing ideas on the immediate problem of how to black out the windows and speculating on the changes that this war was likely to bring to our lives. The changes, on a scale quite bewildering to me, were to come sooner than I could have guessed on that historical Sunday.

2. PRECAUTIONS AND PROPAGANDA

Within what seemed to me to be a remarkably short space of time, I, and every other British citizen, acquired the paraphernalia of wartime. I can remember going with my parents and sister to Holmlea Road School to have our gas masks fitted. We queued. We waited. We moved slowly nearer the desk where some men were standing among piles of small cardboard boxes, which had long loops of string attached. Piles and piles of boxes. Mountains of boxes. And the whole room reeked of rubber, mingled with a hint of school disinfectant from the well-scrubbed floor. I can smell it yet. While we waited in the queue, my father explained that, at all times, we must keep our gas masks within easy reach. The string on the box was a shoulder strap so that we could carry the horrid thing while still keeping our hands free.

At the desk, each head was measured, a mask of the correct size selected and the recipient shown how to put it on. For the first time since war had been declared, I felt frightened. My mask smelt horribly of rubber. When the man helped me to put it on, it clung to the sides of my face like a second skin (as it was designed to do!) and I felt as if I were suffocating. I began to get used to the strange new feeling after a moment or two, but the very act of breathing was hard work. I prayed – yes, I prayed – that I would never have to wear that mask in earnest. The very thought of poison gas held me in a grip of horror.

Grandma had always liked to talk about her youngest son, our Uncle Jim, whom my sister and I had never known. He had been killed in France in 1918, on his way home on leave from his regiment. The troop train was bombed and Jim and his fellow soldiers died – of poison gas. The idea both fascinated and haunted me, but only now did I see the nightmare perhaps becoming reality. Dear God, forbid!

No such horror attended the issue of Identity Card and Ration Book some time afterwards. In fact, I cannot recall being given these. I know that food rationing started in January 1940 and we all had a ration book. I expect that such important documents were handed to my father for the whole family. Receive them we certainly did. The law required it.

All over Britain, people were buying durable covers for their identity cards and even zip-topped waterproof covers for their gas masks. These covers were necessary because it was recognised that Identity Cards and gas masks were going to be around for a long time. A cardboard box with a string loop would not last very long. There was some talk of the war not lasting very long either, even of it being over by Christmas, but few people seemed to believe such tales. "Wishful thinking" they called it. "Wishful thinking", we were told officially, was against the "war effort". These phrases had crept into our every-day vocabulary almost unnoticed.

In one respect, being a child in those early days of wartime was no different from being grown-up. We all, young and old, had to begin at the beginning, learning new words and phrases and a whole new way of living. From walls, a blizzard of posters shouted at us. Reminders were everywhere. "Careless talk costs lives!", "Be brief!" (on the telephone), "Save fuel!", "Dig for Victory!", "Go to it!", "Put that light out!". We needed to be reminded, for it was very difficult at first to assume the sudden disciplines that wartime life demanded of us. For example, it was easy to forget to put the light out before opening an outside door at night. The ensuing shaft of light that cut into the pitch blackness would remind us sharply of our mistake, but not before a voice from the darkness would have bellowed, "Put that light out! Don't you know there's a war on?" We had to be on the alert constantly.

In private houses, shops, offices, and public buildings, blackout material was no sooner purchased than curtains were made and hung in position. They were drab and sombre and, in our house, Mother hung two sets of curtains on every window. The black ones were hung next to the glass and were hidden by the normal, cheerful ones of happier times. We kept our roller blinds as an extra precaution against "showing a light". Crepe paper, coloured very dark green or black, came into its own as a means of reducing the glow from light bulbs. Indoors, half shades were fashioned from the stretchy crepe paper, and hung over existing lamp-shades on the side nearest to the window, or in the case of halls and porches, on the side nearest the outside door. For outdoor use, crepe paper and an elastic band provided effective dimming for hand-held torches. The light from even a small torch could look as bright as a search-light in the all-enveloping darkness of total blackout and all that was permitted was enough light to distinguish kerb stones and similar hazards as one walked by night. The small size of torch, which was not heavy to carry, and which slipped easily into a coat pocket – even a child's coat pocket – was suddenly in heavy demand in shops all over Britain. The bulbs and batteries required – No. 8 batteries – became difficult to find, as people stocked up and the shortage seemed to continue for years.

As my father had explained to me how lights on the ground aided navigation of aircraft overheard I could see why it was important – vital, in fact – to black out windows and all outdoor lights. But I was puzzled by the apparently urgent need for the rolls of sticky tape, which Mother had bought. Certainly I was very pleased when, at last, I was allowed to do something to help, but, when Mother told me what she wanted me to do, I looked at her as if to say, "Are you serious?". She was asking me to stick the tape all over our windows, in a regular lattice pattern about four inches apart. I could not believe my ears. But in those days ten-year-olds did not argue with their elders, especially their parents, and I did as I was asked, keeping my thoughts to myself! As I worked, sticking and snipping, I began to realise that my strange job must be very important, if it made my mother sacrifice her shining windows in such a way. She could never tolerate dirty windows and, as for sticking paper all over them, the very idea must have been anathema to her. Yes, I told myself, there had to be a very good reason for this madness.

When my father came home from work that evening he admired my handiwork. He could hardly avoid noticing it! My trellis work was on display in every room. He could see my bewilderment and took time to explain to me, as gently as he could, about the possibility of air raids with bombs exploding and causing blasts that might easily blow in windows even a long way away. The danger from flying glass would be reduced by my lattice of sticky tape. I was pleased. Later I was to be amazed by the versatility of our various neighbours when they, in their turn, got around to the job of protecting their own windows. Whoever would have guessed at the scope for artistry and imagination provided by such a simple job as taping a window?

If the enemy overhead was to receive no nocturnal help from lights on the ground, neither was the enemy on the ground to receive navigational aid from signposts. This much I discovered when I woke up one morning to find that the big signboard, which had borne the name "Kings Park" in large letters, had been removed from our local railway station, leaving only two widely spaced posts where it had been. I was impressed. Apparently no stone was being left unturned in thwarting the enemy in our midst. The very idea of a spy alighting from our local train and not being able to find out where he was positively delighted ten-year-old me. My imagination, I admit, was coloured by comic papers like *The Dandy* and *The Beano*, which invariably depicted a spy as a shady character equipped with curling moustache, long black cloak and – of course – the spy's stock-in-trade, the smoking onion-bomb!

If signposts were coming down, buildings were going up. Work was going on all over Britain, building shelters, both public – often in Underground stations – and private. Our neighbour, who was a manager with S.C.W.S., had his garage in the back garden replaced by one of the officially approved reinforced brick and concrete shelters, an eye-sore that we had to look upon for years to come. Another neighbour plumped for an "Anderson" shelter, of corrugated iron. He was a dedicated amateur gardener, and I think he chose the "Anderson" type because it could be turfed over and made to blend with the landscape in a way that the brick shelters could never do. Generally speaking, people were allowed to suit themselves about their shelter accommodation. If, they merely wanted to sleep under a stout kitchen table in the basement, they were free to do so. And some did!

My father's solution to the problem was to utilise our basement. Because our house was built on a steep hill, it had a cellar at the back. This was sub-divided into two rooms, a small one under the kitchen where we kept the coal, and a very big one, whitewashed and clean, where garden tools, workbench, deck chairs and all sorts of things were stored. There was enough clear floor space for my sister and me to play there when it rained. As there was electric light and power laid into the cellar, all it needed to make a good air raid shelter was some reinforcement. As my father worked for a firm of steel tube manufacturers, he had no difficulty in having the required number of stout steel props delivered and hammered securely into place, to shore up the cellar. I felt that even if the whole house were to fall down on top of us, those Samsons of steel would not give way.

3. SCHOOL AT HOME AND AWAY

Glasgow Corporation schools were due to re-open for the autumn term soon after the declaration of war. I cannot be absolutely certain of the intended opening date but I think it was to have been 5th September. Usually I willed the summer holidays never to end, for I hated school. But 1939 was different. I was dying for term to start.

The reason for this uncharacteristic keenness on my part was plain curiosity. Our primary school had been a wooden building, put up as a temporary measure to serve the rapidly expanding housing schemes in the Kings Park area until a permanent school could be built. Work on that new building had started some time previously and I and my school mates had stood daily by the boundary fence in Kingsbridge Drive, watching the builders at work. We had to pass the building site on our walk between home and wooden school, so we were able to see the new school grow, from the foundation stage, until the day when the last red-leaded girder was clothed in smooth red bricks and every window was glazed. After the wooden huts, the new building, two storeys high and handsome in red brick and cream roughcast, looked enormous. I could not wait to get inside to see what it was like.

But wait I did. Our school was opened, but its doors were closed to the ordinary children of Kings Park. All unknown to me, people had been working like beavers in the Glasgow Corporation offices, making arrangements to evacuate Glasgow schoolchildren to places of greater safety. Parents had apparently been asked if they wished their children to be evacuated. It transpired that my own parents had opted to keep my sister and me at home with them, so the whole process of evacuation passed over me, unnoticed at the time. My sister kept a scrap-book of newspaper cuttings and I can remember looking through it, much later, and seeing pathetic photographs of evacuees standing in miserable little groups, their belongings at their feet, their gas masks over their shoulders and their identity labels tied firmly in their lapels. Some were taken to Troon, I heard, others farther afield, and some even went, by special arrangement, to Canada.

In the process of screening the potential evacuees there must have been a routine medical examination. Anyway, it was discovered that some children were not immediately suitable for evacuation. There were certain anti-social conditions that had to be eradicated before these children could be admitted to clean foster homes! Some had head lice, others had contagious skin conditions.

I never did know how many centres were opened to clean up these children. I knew only that our new school was commandeered for the purpose and as far as I and my school-mates were concerned our lovely new school building might have been on the moon instead of on top of the hill. Suddenly it was beyond our reach.

The effect of that dramatic change of use was quite drastic. Away back at the planning stage, it had been decided that the new Kings Park school would be allowed to grow into a senior secondary school with a full primary department. The first intake of secondary pupils was due that term, and my sister was to be one of them. So the loss of the building meant that alternative accommodation had to be found for teaching not only an entire primary department but a whole first year intake for the secondary department as well. The new headmaster had a formidable problem to solve.

Before I knew what was happening, my parents, with several others, had offered accommodation to the school. Our house had three bedrooms and by moving my sister into my small room, the largest bedroom became available as a makeshift classroom. The headmaster came to inspect our house to see if it would be suitable. To pass the test, we had to be able to offer, not only a furnished room large enough to conduct classes for about 15 children, but also adequate toilet facilities and an acceptable air raid shelter.

The headmaster went away well satisfied with the facilities that my parents were able to offer. I expect he made many similar visits for inspection, for parents generally were anxious to see resumption of teaching for their children, and many offers of accommodation must have been made.

Priority was given to starting the First Year of the secondary department. As far as I can remember, the pupils were divided into six groups, and each group was allocated to a private house. Our house was one of them. Three groups were to attend classes in the mornings and three in the afternoons. At that stage in the school's development there were only three teachers, and they taught

English, mathematics and French, respectively. Each conducted a lesson in a separate house, then moved on, changing places with one another. The process was repeated at the other three houses in the afternoon. In our own case, the English teacher, Miss Ryan, came first. As she left for her next lesson, Mr Galbraith would arrive to take mathematics and he would depart to be followed by Miss Donachie, the French teacher.

As I was of primary school age, I was still at home all day, waiting for arrangements to be made for my own class. It became my job to open the front door, first to the pupils as they arrived about 1.30pm and then to the teachers as they came and went. I was painfully shy and I hated being on door duty. When news came that my own class was starting at last, I was quite relieved.

My sister was lucky. She did not even need to go to school. School came to her. She did not even have to put on her outdoor shoes, as slippers or gym shoes were worn by all pupils when in the temporary school rooms, by order of the headmaster.

I was less fortunate. My class group was to share two houses, attending each on alternate weeks and although the first house was within 10 minutes walk of my home, the second was much farther away.

To accommodate the secondary class in our house, Mother had removed the bed from the spare room and had borrowed, to replace it, an enormous table, the biggest I had ever seen. Round this, she put every chair we could spare and a few that she had borrowed, to make up the number required by the class. To complete the classroom, my toy blackboard and easel – which was really quite big – stood beside the teacher's chair. The gas fire was enough to heat the room adequately and each pupil brought 2 pence every week towards the cost of the gas.

Things were quite different at the two houses that I had to attend. In both cases the room being used was the sitting room, complete with sofa, armchairs and pouffes, but sadly lacking in tables. We had to put our exercise books on our knees and write as best we could, while our elbows were jogged by the children on either side of us as we sat, squashed together on soft and well-sprung upholstery. The rooms were heated by open coal fires and, because coal was in short supply, it may have been rationed even at that early stage, but I cannot say for certain – we had each to take a big lump of coal to our hostess's house each week. Just imagine me walking more than a mile to "school", carrying my schoolbag on my back, my hated gas mask over my shoulder and a lump of coal in a brown paper parcel! The far-away house seemed even further away on the days when I had to carry the coal. Strangely enough, I always felt a sense of grudge when I handed over my precious lump of coal in that particular house. My hostess usually told me to put it straight on the fire in the living room, where she liked to keep a good, cheerful blaze. But that was her own part of the house. The "school" was conducted in the sitting room and the fireplace there usually held a single, smouldering lump, which was to last all after-noon, giving off little heat and still less cheer.

When I reached home I used to complain to my mother about this apparent unfairness. All I would get in return for my tale of woe was a stiff lecture on how it ill became me to find fault with my hostess when, were it not for her, I would have no school to attend every alternate week!

Because we were receiving part-time education, in my case, afternoons only, the curriculum was cut to the bare essentials. Arithmetic, writing, reading, grammar and spelling seemed to fill our time. We had no "play-time" or interval. Miss Hamilton, our teacher, was careful to give us a task to do while she was out of the room for five minutes having a cup of tea with the lady of the house! It was for our own good, of course, that our noses were kept to the grindstone. But we were too young to appreciate that. It was useless to complain, anyway, for, when we did, the reply was always the same – "Don't you know there's a war on?"

4. JOHN CITIZEN GOES TO IT

Very soon after the war started, my father's employers transferred him to one of their tube-works in Coatbridge. There he was to be Labour Officer and his first assignment was the recruitment of women for work in the shell factory that had been set up, alongside the tube plant. A bitter task it must have been for my father. He had done exactly the same job before, in the days of the war that was supposed to end all wars. He would tell us very little about his job because, as we all knew, careless talk could cost lives.

His transfer to Coatbridge meant that, instead of a twenty minute journey into town on the local train, he had a long, slow, twenty mile journey involving two buses. He had to leave home in the morning before I was up and sometimes he did not get back home until after I was in bed.

The bus services seemed to have been badly hit by the war. I expect it was because many bus crews had been called up for national service and replacements for them were hard to find. In those days, every bus had both a driver and a conductor and it was a case of "men only". Inevitably, before long, there were conductresses on the buses and tramcars. It took some time to get used to seeing women in red and green uniform of Glasgow Corporation Transport but they soon became a familiar part of the wartime scene in the city. One or two of them eventually became drivers, but only of tramcars. I doubt if there was such a thing as a woman bus driver in wartime Glasgow.

Unfamiliar uniforms were cropping up all around us, often being worn by people with far from unfamiliar faces. One of our neighbours, who worked in a Glasgow shipping office, appeared at our door one evening to announce that he was now our local Air Raid Warden. In his new role he looked quite different from his everyday self. An armband was creasing his smart coat-sleeve and his head, which normally wore a black bowler hat, was crowned with a very important looking tin hat wearing the letter "W". He gave us all, children included, a lesson on the use of the stirrup pump and organised a firefighting team, composed of several neighbours.

My father could not be included in this team, because he could not guarantee to be available when required. He and his colleagues at work were on a roster for "firewatching" at the works in Coatbridge. When his turn came, father had to stay overnight on the premises, patrolling, in case of fire. He did not have an armband, but he did have a tin hat, which he brought home one day to show me. I thought it must be great fun to wear one of these and feel important, but I changed my mind when I put father's tin hat on my head. Like the King's crown, it looked very impressive to a spectator, but – oh! – what a weight it was! I was glad to take it off.

Some of the people whom I saw every day, hurrying to catch a train while I was on my way to school, began to appear in uniform. Popular with both men and women was the pale blue battledress of the Royal Observer Corps. The Red Cross seemed well represented among the commuters, too. I even remember seeing a Land Girl in khaki and green, for Kings Park at that time was close to the Glasgow boundary and open farmland. The Land Army was formed, I believe, to help farmers replace labourers who had been called up and to provide extra help to "Dig for Victory" – another slogan of the time.

There were many outlets for helping the war effort, including the W.V.S., still in existence today as the W.R.V.S. And, of course, there was the L.D.V. This was the Local Defence Volunteers, later to have its name changed to the Home Guard and – very much later – thanks to television, to be christened "Dad's Army".

One "army" that helped to win the war wore no uniform. They were the members of the National Savings Groups, which were formed up and down the country, to promote the sale of National Savings stamps and certificates in aid of the war effort. This was something which even children could take part in and my sister and I joined the army of savers. We used to run to the front door when the collector called every Saturday morning. Usually we had sixpence each to spend on a savings stamp. These we licked and stuck into a book and, when we had saved fifteen shillings, we exchanged it for a National Savings certificate.

Our local Savings Group was run by the father of one of my school friends and their house was a hive of activity every Saturday morning with collectors, some of them children, calling to uplift stamps and returning later to hand in the money. Never once did I hear of a collector being molested or robbed. It was just not a done thing, I suppose – against the war effort and all that! We really were a very patriotic people in those days.

5. SEARCHLIGHTS AND SIRENS, BOMBS AND BALLOONS

With the resilience of a normal ten year old, I soon adjusted to my new school life, to my father being away all day, to women doing men's work and to the sight of neighbours in a variety of uniforms. It took me much longer to get used to the blackout.

Because I was attending "school" in the afternoons, it was dark before I got back home. My torch, dimmed with green crepe paper, became as much a part of my normal school equipment as my pencil, ruler and rubber. It was like a friend to me, its muted light guiding me safely along my way. My journey seemed shorter when I could watch the pale blue shafts of searchlights sweeping the sky, crossing and criss-crossing as if in a dance, their bright beams contrasting sharply with the poor light from my torch. The deadly purpose of all this searchlight practice had not yet occurred to me and I looked upon it then as merely a pretty sideshow that the war had introduced. Searchlights made me think, child that I was, of spotlights in a theatre. I still had vivid memories of a scene from a Christmas pantomime that I had been to, the year before, at the

Princess's Theatre: The Thompson Sisters had appeared on stage, wearing silver gowns and, as if by magic, their dresses had changed colour again and again and again. The daughter of the principal comedian of that pantomime was a schoolmate of mine at that time and, in her house, I had met a man who turned out to be the brother of my idols, the Thompson Sisters. He explained to me that his sisters' dress changes were affected by switching the colour of the spotlights. From that day, theatre spotlights had held a magical quality for me and I could not see how searchlights could be any different. It took the Clydebank blitz to bring home to me the terrible truth.

If I thought the searchlights that appeared after dark were dramatic, I thought the barrage balloons that appeared in daylight were ridiculous. They were literally all around us, rising from apparently nowhere to ride, like grey elephants in the sky, tethered by numerous cables. These provided a hazard for enemy aircraft, which were thus obliged to fly higher to avoid the wires. I suppose this made reconnaissance more difficult. It seemed we could have spies in the sky as well as lurking in the holes and corners of the ground. The thought gave me shivers up and down my spine, for flying spies were a new concept, quite unheard of in *The Dandy* and *The Beano*!

Occasionally, but not often enough to be troublesome, we would hear the quite unmistakeable din of a big gun firing in practice. "Anti-aircraft guns" we were told by those who seemed to know about such things. "Ack-ack guns", they were called by those who were really "with it". One boom in particular sounded much nearer than any other and we knew it must come from a gun site close by. Just exactly where it was we had no idea and those of our classmates who did know, because they lived near the site, kept quiet. Careless talk could cost lives and there just might be a spy listening!

Far harder to live with than the booms and bangs of big guns was the sound of the air raid warning. The "alert" siren was an undulating wail that never failed to bring me out in goose pimples, even when it was followed immediately afterwards by the steady note of the "all clear", indicating that it was only a practice.

The first real air raid warning that I can recall occurred on a Saturday afternoon, late in 1940. My father's elder brother, a bachelor, had come to visit us, as was his habit. Saturdays in our house would not have seemed like Saturdays without the presence at the tea table of Uncle John. My sister and I adored him. He was our favourite uncle. As he lived in the country, he liked nothing better than a browse round the shops in Glasgow, especially the gardening and do-it-yourself shops, for he was both a dedicated gardener and a handyman par excellence. He would arrive at our house in time to meet my father coming home from work. (No five day week in those days!) During the course of the afternoon the two men would often take a bus to town, to search for some item that Uncle John needed, but could not buy in his own village. On the day in question, they were bound for Lewis's basement, in Argyle Street. For the handyman this was a real Aladdin's cave, and time flew past unheeded when my uncle was there. Mother was resigned to postponing tea for she knew quite well that, in view of their destination, the men would be later than usual in coming back.

They were, but not for the expected reason. Just as they were making their way to the bus stop for home, the air raid siren wailed the "alert". Quickly and calmly, they and the multitude of shoppers in that part of Argyle Street were shepherded to the nearest public air raid shelter.

Meanwhile, my now very anxious mother was shepherding her two daughters down the back steps to our reinforced cellar. It was the first time we had used it in its dual role as an air raid shelter, and the experience ought to be imprinted on my memory. But it is not. I cannot recall a single thing that the three of us did in the twenty or so minutes that the alert lasted. All I can remember is feeling terribly worried for the safety of my beloved father and uncle, in the city centre.

I never found out whether that alert was a genuine raid or a false alarm. We heard no guns, and when the "all clear" sounded, to release us from the cellar, everything looked normal, not even a searchlight to be seen. The family was reunited shortly afterwards, with the arrival of the next bus from town. Released from recent tension, and once again surrounded by the feeling of security that my father's presence always gave me, I was able to look back on the air raid and think what an anti-climax it had proved to be.

Damp squib or not, that incident made me think for the first time about how war could split up families, a thought that would have struck me earlier had I been evacuated. That brief air raid made me realise how some of my school-friends must feel. For them, separation was not just for the duration of a short air raid, but was constant, because their fathers were young enough to have been called up for National Service. Slowly I was beginning to see the ugliness of war. Rapidly I was growing up.

6. SCHOOL DAYS IN THE SHADOW OF WAR

Eventually King's Park Senior Secondary School was opened for its true purpose and full-time education was restored. The two halves of my class were reunited after having been separated since the end of the summer term 1939. It was by now early 1940, as far as I can recall.

Eagerly anticipated although it had been, that first day in the new building has left me with no special memories. All that remains are vague impressions. Staff and pupils alike, I think, were all touched by the sad thought of what might have been, contrasted with the realities of how things had actually turned out.

The new school was in the shape of a capital E, the legs of the E embracing white concrete playgrounds. But these were choked with clusters of brick and concrete air raid shelters. The school windows that I had watched being glazed, and from which I had longed to admire the view, had been almost blinded by protective net. Whereas at home we had used lattice of sticky tape, the school authorities had covered every square inch of window pane with a fine white mesh, glued to the glass with evil-smelling size. I found this smell quite obnoxious. It seemed to permeate the entire building.

The architects had provided plenty of cloakrooms with neat rows of pegs. But we were forbidden to hang our coats there. Like our gas masks, our outdoor clothing had to be taken wherever we went, in case of a sudden air raid warning, for it was always cold in the unheated shelters. That rule prevailed for the duration of the war and we sat at our desks with our coats across the hinges of our tip-up seats. The assortment of coats, jackets, anoraks and waterproofs, to say nothing of gas mask covers, gave the classrooms an untidy appearance, especially in the case of the senior classes. The bigger the pupil, the longer the coat and some coats inevitably trailed on the floor or cluttered the passages between desks. I am sure the teachers did not like to see a jumble of outdoor clothing in their classrooms. It could not have been very good for the coats, either, and after clothes were rationed, the replacement of a coat cost a lot of precious clothing coupons.

What did hang on the pegs in each cloakroom was a large sack for the collection of waste paper. Rationing of food, clothes, coal, petrol and soap had driven home to us all the importance of avoiding waste of any kind and of making economical use of every resource. Paper could be re-processed and it was easy to collect. Schools did their best to help by putting up sacks and giving pupils a target to aim at. Collection campaigns of various kinds were held from time to time. I can remember taking milk bottle tops, silver paper and foil to school. Kings Park pupils even had a campaign to collect a mile of books, but these were not for salvage.

This collection was organised in the summer of 1942 by a young and enterprising teacher who had joined the English staff. Each year the school roll grew bigger as the secondary department stretched, and every September, when we returned to school after the summer holiday, we found that a few more teachers had been added to the staff to cope with the additional intake of pupils. This particular young man had been a new arrival the previous September and he quickly made his mark. Always interested in psychology, he recognised the plight of troops stationed on lonely sites where action proved to be light and time hung heavy. He saw too that we were all becoming inward looking, depressed by the way that the war seemed to be going. Things looked black then and we were in need of an outside interest to divert our minds. He suggested that we collect books – a whole mile of them – for the troops.

A meticulous house-to-house collection was planned, covering the whole of Kings Park and Croftfoot. Each collector's allotted territory had to be gone over twice. The first visit involved explaining very politely to each householder that we were collecting a mile of books for the troops, and inviting their help. The second visit, a few evenings later, was for the purpose of uplifting the books that had been offered to us. The response was heart warming. We fairly staggered back to the school with the resulting sack loads. The organiser had decided that not only was a mile of books to be collected – it was to be seen to be collected. Senior pupils measured a mile of school corridor and we laid the books along this route so that we could have the satisfaction of seeing our collection. The whole school could watch its progress and help to complete the mile by bringing yet more books. The target was achieved – something like 7,000 books – and many parcels were made up for distribution to troops in isolated outposts, where often the chief enemy was sheer boredom.

That campaign boosted our morale and helped to take our minds off the news bulletins of the day. America had been drawn into the War, Japan had invaded Burma, German troops were advancing in Russia and most of Europe was under German occupation. For those of us who were too young to fight on the war front, it was comforting to know that we could do even a little to help those who were actually in action.

The campaigns to save waste paper and tin-foil were run in conjunction with the City of Glasgow Cleansing Department. The campaign to collect a mile of books was a sole effort by Kings Park School. There were still more campaigns – I suppose they were for propaganda purposes – all concerned with the war in some way or another. Usually they took the form of competitions, either to design a poster or to write an essay. One such campaign was against fire wastage and was sponsored, I believe, by the Caledonian Insurance Company. School children were invited to submit essays on the subject "Fires help Hitler". Even the prizes had a wartime slant to them. My own attempt won Fourth Prize – two National Savings Certificates!

Wartime school life followed as normal a pattern as could be achieved, given the shortage of young teachers due to conscription. In Kings Park School, certain subjects that would have featured on a normal curriculum could not be taught during the war because fully qualified teachers of these subjects simply were not to be found. I had reached Fourth Year of secondary school before a specialist geography teacher was engaged and for long periods we were without staff qualified to teach Higher German, Higher history and Higher Latin. The Scottish Senior Leaving Certificate examinations were modified during the war years and papers were set on a regional basis instead of a national one. University courses were also abbreviated for the duration of the war. I am sure that some of the first batch of pupils to sit the "Highers" in Kings Park – some of those who started first year in our houses – entered Glasgow University and graduated M.A. in the space of two years.

Class numbers were bigger during the War than would be allowed today. They had to be. There were not always enough teachers to permit the luxury of smaller classes. Discipline did not appear to suffer, for the war seemed to give us all a sense of responsibility and pupils generally realised that their teachers were under strain. We all pulled together, for the sake of the war effort. I know of one thing, and one thing only, that brought the class work in Kings Park School to a complete halt in wartime. It happened almost every day, sometimes several times a day. Fortunately, the hiatus was brief, usually only a minute or so. But it was effective. Noise – an ear-splitting racket – would drown all other sound. Even if a teacher had shouted he would have been wasting his breath. Pupils would have needed to have been able to lipread to interpret his words. The human voice was no match for a convoy of tanks! We did the only thing we could do in the circumstances. We put our fingers in our ears and waited patiently for the tanks to pass.

Somewhere in Glasgow there was a factory where army tanks were either built or repaired. It was not my business to know the details. Careless talk could cost lives! What the residents of Kings Park could not possibly fail to know was that these tanks were tested, two and three at a time, on a route that included the entire length of Kings Park Avenue. When they came roaring and clanking and squeaking up the steep hill, ornaments shook, windows rattled, some householders claimed that cracks appeared in walls – and teachers were temporarily silenced. But we grew accustomed to this phenomenon, as we did to all else that had once seemed strange. However, I never felt happy if I happened to be walking down the Avenue when a convoy of tanks roared past. There was such a thing as being too close for comfort!

Throughout the war years, schools had air raid warning drills much as they have fire drill in peacetime. We would grab our gas masks and coats and walk – not run – to the shelter allotted to our class. As far as I can remember, there was only one actual air raid during school hours and I was in primary school at the time. It must have been early in 1941. I have a clear memory of sitting with other pupils on the slatted wooden bench that ran all around the inside wall of the brick shelter, the cold from the wall seeping into our backs, while the teachers stood in worried conversation.

An impromptu concert was held, with no shortage of volunteers to sing solos. We had several really good singers in our class. One of these, a girl called Anne, who was a devoted fan of Deanna Durbin, sang "Waltzing High in the Clouds". Other favourites that we all joined in were "Run Rabbit Run" and "Over the Rainbow". My heart still thumps when I hear these songs today.

7. YES, WE HAVE NO BANANAS

The *S.S. Athenia* was sunk by a German submarine – "U-boats", we learned to call them – on the very day that war was declared. It took a while for the news to sink into my mind. The whole concept of a passenger liner going down was new to me. With all the faith of a child, I had, until then, taken for granted that, when one boarded a ship, be it Clyde steamer or Atlantic liner, one automatically arrived safely at one's destination. The thought of the boat sinking beneath my feet had never even faintly occurred to me. But there was no escaping from this brutal fact that the Germans had sunk a British liner full of innocent people. Over a hundred passengers had been lost. The war was not of their making. Why should they have to die? And on a Sunday, too! I found the whole incident quite repugnant. My parents were shocked by the news, of course, but I think they accepted the hard fact without the sense of disbelief that I had felt initially. They seemed to have lived through something similar in the Great War. They talked about the *Lusitania*, and sighed as if the memory were painful.

We were to hear a great deal more about U-boat attacks on our shipping during the next five years. Suddenly, our merchant fleet was in the forefront of battle. The Royal Navy did what it could to protect the cargo ships but, at first, our losses of ships, cargoes and men were very heavy. Convoys were made up and these sailed zigzag courses under Naval escort. But the U-boats hunted under the water and picked off their vulnerable targets mainly by night. Newspapers carried harrowing stories of survivors enduring days and weeks in open boats before being picked up. There was not a soul in Britain who did not admire the men of our Merchant Navy. At school we had learned a song, "Caller Herrin", which, in one verse, refers to the fish as "lives o' men". We were all beginning to realise that not just herring, but all our imported food, fuel oil for 'planes and tractors and raw material for our factories were being paid for by the lives of our sailors. We could see that shortages were inevitable and that the only way to overcome this was to ration what we had. Priority for the most pressing need and fair shares for all became the accepted dictum. Knowing why rationing was necessary seemed to make it much easier to bear.

It was no surprise when food rationing was introduced at the beginning of 1940. Everyone had a Ration Book and each book had pages of coloured coupons for the various commodities on ration. Customers were required to register with a shop of their choice for each rationed item and the name and address of the shop had to be filled in, once for each commodity, in every book in the household. My father took on the job of form filling. It was a tedious task and when I was a bit older I was given this duty each time we had to re-register. Some shopkeepers had rubber stamps made, the size of the spaces in the ration books and they gladly stamped their names and addresses for their customers, thereby saving a great deal of work. That must have been an especial help to old people whose hands were shaky or whose sight was not good.

Exactly which items were rationed and how much of each we were entitled to has long since faded from my mind. I do know that bacon, butter, cheese, eggs, meat, sugar and soap were rationed. Oddly enough, bread was not rationed until after the war was over! Cereals like barley, rice and lentils were not rationed, as far as I can recall and neither were potatoes and other vegetables, unless by seasonal scarcity. Gradually, new items were added to the list of rationed goods and spare pages at the back of the ration books coped with these.

In 1941, dress materials, household linen and clothing – except hats, I believe! – were rationed, batches of clothing coupons being issued to each person and a coupon value given to every article. If one bought, say, a pair of shoes, the appropriate number of coupons had to be surrendered. As X coupons had to last for Y months, impulse buying became a thing of the past! One had to plan one's purchases of clothing very carefully, and as for dishtowels, sheets, etc. drastic economies had to be practised. We patched and darned as we had never done before in my life time. "There's no shame in a neat patch", Mother would say. I was always a good darner and throughout the years of rationing I had the job of darning family socks that had holes in them!

Food was rationed by quantity, except butcher meat, which was rationed by price. We were all entitled to buy meat each week up to a certain value. For a time the ration was 1s 2d (6p), which seems quite incredible today. I think the figure varied occasionally if the Minister of Food felt the national meat situation merited an adjustment. Offal was not rationed and perhaps corned beef was off ration too? It certainly figured hugely in our menus, but maybe it was merely inexpensive and thereby yielded a good return for one's precious one-and-tuppence worth.

Mother clung to her peacetime habit of having a Sunday joint. It would have taken more than Adolf Hitler to change that. Perhaps the "joint" might be more correctly described as a "piece of meat", but no matter, by skilful judgement Mother managed to continue to serve a "joint" hot on Sundays, cold on Mondays and, if it stretched, maybe even shepherd's pie or stovies on Tuesdays. I have a vivid memory of Mother, one Sunday at dinnertime, ceremonially carrying the "joint" to the table on a saucer! She gave her big, oval meat-plates – which we called ashets – to a Boy Scout jumble sale, for I think she felt she would never again have a piece of meat big enough to serve on an ashet.

Mother, like all her sister housewives, had to employ great ingenuity in planning nutritious meals for the family. She managed remarkably well. Good, nourishing, homemade soup always seemed to be available in our house. Rabbits, for delicious stews, were plentiful in those wartime days long before myxomatosis. I used to think that anyone who had not tasted the rich gravy of a rabbit stew had not lived. Oatmeal was a splendid source of protein and Mother used it a lot since meat, cheese and eggs were rationed. We were fortunate enough never to be without an onion in the house and Mother often made skirlie, an old Scots dish, with dripping, onion, oatmeal, salt and pepper. Served with mashed potato and washed down with milk, it made a hearty meal.

The uses of corned beef were legion and the Ministry of Food – another creation of wartime – was always publishing new ways of serving it. They had a five minute programme on the wireless in the mornings, after the eight o'clock news called *On the Kitchen Front*, with well-known broadcasters like the late Freddie Grisewood giving recipes that were new, interesting and within the scope of wartime shopping. Mother was a regular listener and at least one recipe that she picked up from that programme became a family favourite. It was called "sapper's savoury" and consisted of corned beef dressed up in a curry sauce, with cooking apple and onion. Very warming it was, to come home to on a cold day.

The Ministry of Food took advertising space in the national Press to publish a regular series of food bulletins, with economical recipes and suggestions for making the most of the food rations. With the nation's health in mind, these bulletins encouraged us to eat plenty of carrots, because- they assured us – carrots helped us to see in the dark! To ensure an even higher intake of vitamin C, we were further exhorted to eat plenty of potatoes. To this end, we were introduced to a most engaging little fellow, called (I think!) "Potato Pete", who looked like a distant relative of Humpty Dumpty. He had an infectious smile and always seemed to be popping up in the papers with more and still more recipes using potatoes.

To my knowledge, there was no shortage of potatoes during the war. They were easy to grow and were to be found in nearly every garden. Some people who were keen on gardening, and had time to spare, took over allotments and planted these with vegetables. This was a real test of physical fitness, for the allotments were often won by hard labour from virgin ground. I knew some residents of Kings Park who actually cultivated the railway embankment during the war, with the blessing of the L.M. & S. Railway Company. It was all part of the war effort.

Shortages were inevitable and some were felt more acutely than others, onions, for instance. But, generally speaking, we learned to overcome shortages by using substitutes, like saccharin instead of sugar. Or we simply did without. "Tighten your belts", the Minister of Food told us… And we did.

One of the most ingenious substitutes dreamed up during the war was "Mock Banana"! The banana was one fruit that simply disappeared from Britain during the war. Small children grew up not knowing what a banana tasted like. Scarcity seemed to lend desirability and people hankered for the taste and smell of a banana, even for the feel of its texture on the tongue. Bottles of banana flavouring were readily obtainable in grocer's shops. A few drops added to a homemade sponge cake, or to the icing if one could spare the sugar, was enough to trigger nostalgic reminiscences of the simple pleasure to be found in unzipping a banana! The boffins at the Ministry of Food must have been working hard in the official kitchens behind the scenes. Perhaps it was deemed necessary for the upkeep of the nation's morale that an acceptable banana substitute be found! Anyway, the day eventually dawned when we opened our newspapers to find the latest Ministry of Food bulletin announcing triumphantly "Banana Cream". We tried it. I think the whole nation tried it! And it worked. Not only did it resemble the taste of the real article, but it echoed the texture and colour, too. It scored a real triumph and came as a boon to hard-pressed mothers who were trying to cater for children's parties. It gave them back that old stand-by, the banana sandwich.

How was it done? The answer lay in the homegrown parsnip! One took as much sugar and margarine as one could spare from the ration, in equal quantities, and beat them to a cream. A parsnip was boiled till tender, thoroughly mashed and, when cold, added to the creamed fat and sugar. A few drops of banana flavouring – not too much and not too little – were added and the whole thing beaten together until thoroughly blended. Abracadabra – banana cream!

Oddly enough, when the first consignment of genuine bananas reached the shops just after the war, some of the seven year olds and younger who had never been able to taste the fruit and who knew of it only from picture books and hearsay, found to their acute disappointment that they did not like bananas after all!

If it were possible for my children's generation to take a backwards trip through time and go shopping in the years of rationing, they wouldn't recognise some of the most common items on the shelves in the grocer's shop. Anonymity seemed to be the order of the day. Brand names disappeared from many items. Butter – all butter – was "National Butter". Margarine, except the kosher variety, was "Special Margarine". Its plain wrappers boasted that the contents included vitamins A and D. The brand name remained a mystery. Cheese was as anonymous as the butter and margarine, but the ration for non-manual workers was so small that it did not really matter whether it was cheshire, cheddar, dunlop or common "mouse-trap". It was eaten so quickly that it was a case of "Now you see it, now you don't". People whose jobs involved heavy physical labour, like miners and agricultural workers, qualified for additional cheese, on the grounds that they needed extra protein and that cheese was a convenient food for the packed lunches that these jobs usually demanded.

White bread was not white during the war. It was more of a dirty grey. And a big brown loaf was introduced, with the highly original name, "National Loaf".

Eggs were in such short supply that dried egg was put on the market, to supplement the ration. I have not seen packets of dried egg since rationing ended. I am not sorry. It was not high on my list of favourite wartime food. "Reconstitute" was another new word in the nation's vocabulary. Dried egg had to be reconstituted by whisking cold water into the yellow powder. The result was supposed to be just like freshly whisked eggs. But achieving that result was not as easy as it sounds. In these days, the average house-wife did not have access to sophisticated kitchen aids, like electric food mixers and liquidisers. We had to use a one-woman-powered whisk or fork. And such tools were scarcely adequate to cope with such a temperamental product as dried egg. It tended to be lumpy, obstinately lumpy, a challenge to the cook, who was left to grit her teeth and swear to beat dried egg before it beat her. Even when a smooth mix was achieved, the cooked end product tended to be disappointing. Unless carefully watched while cooking, a dried egg omelette could be leathery in texture. Still, it was better than nothing. Mother liked to bake with dried egg, because it could be sifted with the dry ingredients. I always preferred it like that.

It was typical of the British sense of humour that jokes were made about every aspect of rationing and shortages. On the wire-less, comedians such as the late Rob Wilton kept up our spirits by poking fun at genuine bugbears like queuing, the blackout, scarcity of things like No 8 torch batteries, onions and bananas, and – inev-itably – dried egg. They helped us to see the lighter side of some very dark days.

8. QUEUE HERE!

Depending on one's attitude to standing in the inevitable queue, shopping in wartime could be either a wearisome bore or a social occasion. There was no escape from the queue. It was a built-in discipline of wartime living. As the alternative was a free-for-all scramble, the British accepted the queue as the only civilised procedure. It became a habit, with its own code of ethics. First come, first served, was the accepted rule. A verbal roasting was the least that anyone rash enough to try queue-jumping could expect from those legally in front of him. Jumping the queue was simply not the done thing. Looking back, I get the impression that we queued for absolutely everything, whether it was at the bus stop, the grocer's, the baker's, the butcher's, the fishmonger's, the bank, or the cinema.

We knew when we set off on a shopping expedition that no sooner would we have reached the head of the queue in the first shop than we would have to join the tail of the queue in the second. The only difference would be that the shopping bag would be heavier to carry during the second wait, and so on until, by the third or fourth spell of queuing, the shopping bag, now too heavy to hold, would be lying at our feet and it, and the bags of other similarly laden shoppers, would present obstacles for customers to negotiate on their way out of the shop. Many a time, after having been served at last, I picked and jostled my way from shop counter to shop door, high-stepping over other people's bags, my own bulging holdall held high before me. This feat of strength served two purposes. It saved those still queuing from being brushed or bruised by my heavy leather bag, or – even worse – having their precious stockings laddered, and it acted for me like a bulldozer, clearing a path to the exit.

Obviously, wartime shopping put a heavy strain on women like my mother – strain that was at the time physical and mental. While she endured the long periods of standing, slowly shuffling nearer the top of the queue, she was busy planning, revising and re-planning in her head how to use her coupons and cash to the best advantage. The points system allowed certain elasticity and gave freedom of choice within the limits set in each rationing period. It worked for certain items of foodstuffs in the way that clothing coupons controlled purchases of clothing and household linen. If the shopper decided to buy a tin of Spam, which cost a lot of points, she had to restrict her purchases of other items that were "on points", like dried fruit, tinned fruit, etc. It was no use – pointless, in fact – asking the shopkeeper for a large tin of pears if insufficient points remained to cover that purchase. Even if there were pounds, shillings and pence in the purse, without points these were nothing.

I really believe that the treadmill of queuing, rationing and juggling with points, week in, week out, in all weathers, with only an indifferent public transport service to help carry the load home would have broken the morale of the British housewife, but for the social side of the queue. People in queues do tend to talk to one another, even if they are total strangers. That has always been my experience in warm-hearted Glasgow and I am sure it holds good elsewhere, too. Our local shops became a kind of social centre where women could meet each other and talk as they queued, sharing the worries of wartime and, perhaps, in so doing, lightening each other's load. Nowadays, they do that kind of thing, sitting idly at pre-arranged coffee mornings. But during the war there was not the time to spare for such luxuries. "See you at Willie's!" meant, "I'll see you in the queue at the fish-mongers on Saturday morning!"

When my children think of a queue today, they get a picture in their minds of people with baskets and trolleys, standing in a more or less straight line at the checkout of a supermarket, with space around them to allow free movement by other shoppers. Some people grumble if the delay is more than a few minutes. It never seems to occur to them to count their modern blessings. Because they are in an up-to-date supermarket, they have been able to buy groceries, butcher meat, milk, fruit and vegetables and fish in one swift, self-service operation and, further, having passed through the checkout after only one spell of queuing, they are free to go home, usually by car. This generation of shoppers would not recognise the grocer's shop with which my mother was registered during the war. (To be strictly accurate, I should say "shops", because one was allowed to change shops at the beginning of a new rationing period, if one wished to do so, and an occasional change was as good as a tonic.)

When food rationing was introduced in 1940, Mother decided to register with the grocer's shop that was within walking distance of our house. It happened to be a branch of the Kinning Park Co-operative Society. At that time, they employed a message boy, whose name was Jackie, and he would deliver our groceries on his big, black bicycle with the deep wicker basket in front. This luxury turned out to be of brief duration. Jackie left the service of the Co-op when he was accepted as an apprentice pattern maker at John Brown's shipyard and he was not replaced. We missed him. He was a cheerful lad with a happy smile. Thereafter, my sister and I were roped in, to help carry the groceries home and one or other of us usually accompanied Mother to the shop, or, in later years, went by ourselves.

The shop was small, quite cramped by today's standards, and I stood in tight-packed U-shaped queues in it for seemingly interminable hours, over the years. I can see it in my mind's eye yet, just as I can feel the sawdust under my feet. It was not only public houses and butchers' shops that put sawdust on the floor!

Supermarkets and self-service grocers' shops were not to be found in those days. Shops employed shop assistants to give personal service at the counter. At our local grocer's shop there were three or four assistants, who stood behind a long, marble-topped counter. Behind them, from floor to ceiling, the entire wall space was taken up by laden shelves. A ladder leaned there, ready for use in reaching the top-most shelves. At one end of the counter, there was a ham slicing machine and a set of scales with brass weights. Beside that, on the cold marble counter, was a big slab of National butter, with two ribbed, wooden butter patters in a stone jar of cold water alongside. Then came a whole cheese, of whatever variety that happened to be available, with a wire cheese cutter. A neat pile of greaseproof paper, cut into quite small pieces, lay ready to wrap the meagre portions as the rations for each customer were cut on demand.

The assistants were too busy to take cash and issue change. There was a lady cashier to do that. She sat in a little pulpit-like office, on the customers' side of the counter, high and lifted up. Money scudded from counter to cashier and back again by overhead wires. These carried small cylinders, made of wood and brass, with screw tops. The customers' cash having been put into one of these, a sharp tug on a rope sent the cylinder with surprising speed directly to the cashier's hand. Any change returned in the same way. I used to while away the time just watching this shuttle service.

When, at last, my turn came to be served, I felt stupidly self-conscious and overcome by shyness. The procedure was that, as soon as one assistant because free, the next person in the queue squeezed over to the space at the counter and began rhyming off the grocery order. I was so self-conscious that I hated speaking loudly in the shop. With the tail of the queue pressing behind me, (for it snaked up the counter and back down again, sometimes out to the pavement), I always had the feeling that the experienced shoppers standing at my back were listening to my every request and waiting for me to make a mistake. In fact, they were usually so busy chatting that they probably never noticed me. But I was too nervous to think of that. Children of my generation had less self-confidence than their modern counter-parts seem to have.

A lot of time and energy was spent by the shop assistant in fetching and carrying each requested item to the counter, where it was piled in front of the customer. Some commodities, like the rations of butter, bacon and cheese, had to be specially cut, then scrupulously weighed, wrapped and priced. In search of other requested articles, the harassed assistant would scuttle about, diving under the counter, shinning up the ladder or opening crates in the back shop. The order complete, the coupons had to be cancelled and the appropriate points cut out. Each assistant had a pair of scissors hanging on a string from the belt of her overall, for this purpose. Once the coupons and points had been dealt with, the cost of the order would be worked out. Taking a pencil from her pocket – we had no ball-point pens then! – the assistant would list the price of every item in the grocery pile. This was usually scribbled on a paper bag! The addition sum would be done and, if the customer disagreed with the arithmetic, it was done again. Then, and only then, cash changed hands, the shopping bag was packed and the customer thankfully made her way through the throng, into fresh air.

If a shop received a consignment of something that was in short supply, that article would be put on sale to "registered customers only". I can remember a boy, called Alf, who lived in Kings Park. His mother and father both did war work and were out all day. Alf and his four brothers shared the household chores and Alf's task was the Saturday shopping. With practice, he reduced the spending of his family's points allocation to a fine art. He became a skilled shopper, with an almost uncanny knack of knowing which shops had special treats on offer to their registered customers. Using his bicycle, he could dash from one shop to another, and he had the "Open Sesame" to a surprising number of grocers. "Registered customers only" was no barrier to him, for, coming from a large family, he had taken the precaution of registering different members of his family in different shops! He could truthfully claim to be a registered customer in about five different grocers' shops, all quite near each other in the Mount Florida area. As time was not important to him – for he had all Saturday at his disposal – Alf seldom failed to turn up trumps when he returned home on Saturdays with some rare treat that he had ferreted out while on his shipping rounds. But he was sorely disappointed on one occasion. Flushed with triumph after being allowed to buy one orange in a shop where he had stood in a queue for a long time, he had pedalled quickly for home. It mattered little that each member of his family would perhaps get only one segment as their share of the precious fruit. It was the taste that was important, for he could not remember when he had last been lucky enough to get an orange. Alas, within sight of home, his string shopping bag had slipped sideways from its place behind the saddle of his bicycle and, in a trice, the back wheel had trapped the mesh of the bag. There was only one casualty – the hard-won orange. It was sadly squashed. And that was how poor Alf felt, too.

9. THE BLITZ

For many people who were civilians during the war, one of their outstanding memories of that time is of the 1940/41 blitz. But not for me. Although I have the clearest recollection of quite minor events that took place earlier than that time, my memory of the actual attack on Clydebank is muzzy. I suppose I should be grateful, for those nights are not pleasant to recall.

"Blitz" was a word that entered our vocabulary of everyday speech early in the war. Of German derivation, it was an abbreviation of "blitzkrieg" meaning "lightning war". When the German plans to invade Britain in 1940 were thwarted by the Battle of Britain, Hitler resorted to air raids by night on cities throughout Britain. London was the first to suffer and we all realised that it was only a matter of time before Glasgow was made a target. Precisely when we could expect an attack was anyone's guess and we had to be ready. This watching and waiting and wondering was a deliberately imposed strain on the nerves of the British people and part of the enemy plan for lowering the nation's morale.

When Glasgow's turn for bombing came, in March 1941, we had little or no sleep for several nights in succession. I think that is why my memory is blurred. Healthy eleven-year-olds need a good night's sleep and I was no exception to this rule. I lived through the broken nights of the blitz like the dormouse in *Alice in Wonderland*.

I remember lying in bed in the dark and hearing a noise. I remember the dawning realisation that this was not a dream. I was awake and the noise was the "alert". The bedroom light was snapped on and Mother threw my clothes on the bed and helped me put them on. My limbs felt heavy and I was incapable of hurrying. My sister was ready before me and Father led her out of the house and down the back stairs, to the cellar. Mother followed with me, when I was ready. She had to hold my arm as we went down the stairs, for, in my sleepy state, I was staggering. The night sky was illuminated with cold blue searchlights, but, for me, these had suddenly lost their magic. They were searching for enemy planes and that was starkly real.

As soon as we were all inside the cellar, my father closed the door and drew the curtain across it, to exclude draughts and chinks of light. It was then safe to switch on the light. The sudden brightness helped to waken me up and I was able to lend a hand in converting the cellar into as cosy a shelter as we could make it. We opened up four deckchairs and a small picnic table. The one-kilowatt electric fire was plugged in and we settled down, the chairs in a semicircle facing the door. I do not remember when the guns started firing. The barrage seemed to go on and on and on. When the house shook, we knew that our local anti-aircraft gun had started firing. Its report was deafening, far louder than anything I had ever heard before, so loud that the noise seemed to hurt.

I have no idea of how long we were shut in the cellar. I think I dozed a bit, in between thundering bangs. Strangely enough, I do not remember feeling frightened. I know that I felt cold. The cellar was warm, but lack of sleep made me shiver. I remember being led back to bed when the "all clear" sounded and, in what seemed to me like next to no time, Mother's alarm clock was bidding us all get up. Mother was unsure of what to do about sending us to school that morning. She felt that we would be the better for a long lie in bed, but, in the absence of instructions from the headmaster to guide her, she decided to obey the law and send us to school, as usual.

Off we went, my sister and I, up the hill to school, with our schoolbags and gas masks. A group of teachers was waiting at the main door, to assess the number of children who would turn up that morning. When the nine o'clock bell rang, there were less than forty of us in the whole school. We were all sent into one classroom and a teacher stayed with us to supervise us. I remember her telling us that we were all brave little soldiers for reporting for class after such a night!

The remainder of the pupils arrived for classes in the afternoon and, before we were dismissed at four o'clock, the headmaster issued clear instructions for use in the event of any future nocturnal air raid. If the "all clear" sounded before 2am, we were to report to school at 10am the following day; if the "all clear" sounded after 2am, we were to take the following morning off. We all hoped we would never have to implement these rules, but in fact, they were to be applied that very night, and maybe on the next night, too. The whole blitz seemed to go on for a long time, one night merging with another, but the memory of a sleepy child is not reliable.

When the wail of the "alert" roused me on the second night, I was much better prepared for action than I had been on the first night. The whole family seemed to be in the shelter in record time. Maybe it was because the guns were already barking. I can remember on at least one night during the blitz, going back to bed after the "all clear", only to be re-awakened soon afterwards by the "alert". That was when we seemed to be in the cellar for most of the night. Mother had taken the electric kettle down with her and she made a pot of tea. I expect she made several pots of tea before the dawn broke.

The atmosphere in our cellar grew very heavy. Ventilation was a problem because we dared not show chinks of light. My father had been holding me on his knee to soothe me into some kind of sleep. He had succeeded and I had slept for almost two hours. When I woke up, I was stiff and poor, uncomplaining Father was almost rigid with cramp. A sleeping eleven-year-old is no light weight. To stretch his aching limbs, Father decided to go outside for a little while. We put the light out for a second, to allow him to open the door. A welcome breath of fresh night air came into the cellar as Father went out.

Several neighbours had the same idea and Father found some relief from tension in chatting to these men. They kept their voices low, for at night, sounds travels far and even a whisper seems to carry a long way. As there seemed to be a lull in overhead activity, Father allowed us all to take turns in standing with him in the back porch, breathing the cool air, which bore the strange smell of cordite, and watching the occasional flashes of searchlights. Away to the west, down river, the sky had a dull, red glow. The guns had fallen silent, but we waited in vain for the "all clear". During my spell in the porch with Father, we heard a new sound, a distinct whine. Then came a "crump" and another sound, which I recognised at once. It was the unmistakable noise of bricks falling. Many a time I had stood beside lorries tipping loads of bricks when the new school was going up. The sound was identical. But, this time, it was of a building coming down.

We digested this new fact and felt cold shivers of horror. Remembering how sound carries at night, Father said the bomb had dropped farther away than I seemed to think. When a bright red glow appeared in the sky soon afterwards, I knew that he was right. It must have been more than a mile away. I scuttled back to the cellar, for I knew that Mother would be getting very anxious. Down there, with the door shut, she and my sister had heard the bricks fall and, when I told them about the bomb, Mother was appalled to think that I had been out of the shelter at the time. That was the last time my sister and I were allowed out during an air raid!

As the "all clear" did not sound until well after 2am, the whole school had the morning off. Most of the children, like my sister and me, lay in bed until mid-morning and then began to pick up the strands of life again. It is quite amazing how sleep refreshes young bodies and minds. Every child in the district appeared to be out, searching for souvenirs, before noon. Those who were lucky enough to own bicycles did tours of reconnaissance and the rest of us were all positively anxious to get back to school in the afternoon, to catch up on their news!

The cycling scouts duly reported, in awed tones, that direct hits had been scored on an empty Church near Victoria Road and on a house in Boyd Street. This must have been where I had heard the bricks falling. Trophies were produced and compared. We all seemed to have our share of narrow aluminium strips, which were found festooning the garden railings of Kings Park when daylight broke. And one or two boys proudly displayed wicked-looking pieces of shrapnel. When I saw the jagged edges, I began to understand why Wardens and Home Guards wore tin hats during an air raid.

There was much that we did not find out just then. It would not have been good for us to know the full horror that had struck Clydebank area during those nights. We, in Kings Park, had been merely on the fringe of its ferocity and we were among the lucky ones. My memories are muzzy and I want to keep them that way. I know I could discover the precise dates, duration and other dreadful details of the blitz by searching in the official records of the war. I choose not to do so. There are some memories that should be allowed quietly to fade.

10. HOLIDAYS

Holidays were considered to be a great luxury during the war. When taken at all, they were usually spent at home. A wide area of Scotland was a "Restricted Zone", where a permit was required for entry. The permit was issued only if there was a very good reason for wanting it and "holidays" did not qualify as a good enough reason! Travel was essentially by public transport. Because petrol was rationed, pleasure motoring was almost non-existent. Any private motorist foolhardy enough to attempt to take petrol from the tank of a vehicle using the "commercial" variety ran the risk of being found out, because the commercial petrol was coloured pink! Travellers had a choice of bus, bicycle or train – steam train, of course. Delays were commonplace, vehicles could be cold and draughty and travel in the blackout was miserable. Desirable prerequisites were an inexhaustible patience and a strong constitution. It was little wonder that so few people on holiday seemed prepared to make the effort to go away.

I grew well used to "holidays at home" and time never seemed to drag. There was plenty to do, either helping with the shopping –

often a long, slow business because of queues and coupons – or doing my bit in the garden, helping to "Dig for Victory".

From 1939 until 1945, we had just one real holiday as a family, when we were away from home together for a week. It was in the dark days of 1941. My sister had been ill and the doctor prescribed a change, to buck her up. Father arranged to take a week's leave and all four of us went, by bus, to the village of Lesmahagow in Lanark-shire. Being in the tomato and soft fruit growing area, it was a real change from Glasgow, although it was not very far away. For me, the excitement of going on holiday was heightened by the know-ledge that I was being kept off school for the purpose, although it was my sister and not I who was ill. The school Attendance Officer, Mr Barrie, would have something to say to my parents about that when I got back, I felt sure.

Alex, one of my grown-up cousins, lived in Lesmahagow, where he had his own baker's shop. He recommended the Commercial Hotel and booked us in there. When we arrived, he introduced us to the proprietrix, Mrs Gilbert, who made us feel very welcome. The Hotel proved to be comfortable and small enough to be really homely. We were the only guests apart from three sisters from the Channel Islands. They had made the Hotel their temporary home, after fleeing from their native Jersey, just before the German inva-sion in 1940.

In the course of our week's stay, I overcame my shyness suffi-ciently to tell these ladies about four new girls who had joined my class at school. They too, were Channel Islanders and were among a large number of refugee children who had been given foster homes in the Kings Park area. The sisters were interested to hear about this link with home and they asked me lots of questions. I remember telling them that the Channel Island children did not seem to be as good at sums as their Glasgow counterparts, but, when it came to knitting, they were well ahead of us. All four new girls in my class could knit very fast and accurately and, while the rest of us were still laboriously making kettle-holders and hot water bottle covers, they were knocking up skirts and jumpers, in record time! It did not escape my notice that, in the evenings, as the guests sat in the hotel lounge, the three sisters also knitted dexterously and I wondered if island life automatically produced good knitters. After all, Fair Isle, the Shetlands and the Arran Isles were famous for that very thing.

Knitting was not the only skill that our fellow guests displayed. One proved to be a competent pianist and another sang. They were a jolly trio and good company. As my cousin Alex was a tenor soloist of semi-professional standard, we were treated to a series of musical evenings throughout that week. The lounge boasted a piano, but no radio. Transistors had not yet been heard of in civilian life and, with no wireless set, we could hear no news bulletins. For us, for a precious week, the war was shut out.

Alex showed us round the bakehouse at the back of his shop and we savoured the glorious, all-pervading smell of newly baked bread. Like most small family bakers at that time, Alex made his own bread and this was the linchpin of the business. (After the war, the big, city-based chains began delivering their mass-produced loaves to shops all over the country and thus deprived many small bakers, not only of their own bread, but of their "bread and butter".)

On the shop half-day, Alex took us all to visit some friends of his who were tomato growers on quite a large scale. The pungent smell of ripe Scotch tomatoes hung in the glasshouses as heavily as did the smell of bread in the bakehouse. I loved it. But what made the biggest impression on my young mind was not the trusses of ripe tomatoes, nor the steamy heat of the glass-houses, but the glass itself. There was not an inch of sticky tape or evil-smelling net to be seen. What would happen if a bomb dropped, I wondered. But I was too shy to ask.

Looking back on that holiday, it seems to be summed up by a series of nostalgic smells. There was the – to me – unaccustomed whiff of spirits from the Hotel Bar, drifting upstairs to the lounge; the beckoning aroma of bacon and egg every morning, rationing or not; the newly baked bread of the bakehouse; the damp earth and ripe tomatoes; and the mustiness of Joe's Antique shop.

Joe's shop was next door to Alex's bakery and we often called to see him. His premises were so cluttered that I marvelled that he ever found anything when he was asked for it. He seemed to sell anything and everything. My sister and I had a lot of fun simply poking about in the dark corners among the dust-laden stock. The musty smell of mildew was quickly dispelled once we were back in the sunshine of the pavement outside. The sun seemed to shine for us, all week long.

During that holiday, one incident occurred that I simply did not understand. Today's eleven year olds would not have been so ignorant! We had returned to the Hotel for our evening meal and Mrs Gilbert was waiting for us. She hurried to greet us with the news of a strange coincidence. A middle aged couple had booked in for that night and when the gentleman had signed the visitors' book, what would his address be but Kings Park, Glasgow! Mrs Gilbert was all agog with her news. Did we know the newcomers, she wondered. When my parents heard the name and address, they found that they did indeed know the couple. The lived quite near us, in fact. Quite delighted, Mrs Gilbert arranged to put the new couple at our table, so that we could have a chat over the meal.

In due course, the dinner gong sounded. The four of us were first to reach the dining room. When the door opened, shortly afterwards, my parents rose to greet their acquaintances. But the outstretched hands dropped and even I, in my innocence, could feel the atmosphere solidify. That meal nearly choked us all. I thought it would never end. And I could not figure out what was the matter. I was very much older when my mother eventually explained to me that the gentleman was indeed Mr X from Kings Park, but the lady was most certainly not Mrs X! That couple took an early breakfast next day and were gone before we were up. I never saw them again. Who could have imagined that such skeletons lurked in the respectable cupboards of Kings Park!

That was the first and last proper holiday together that our family had in wartime. But we were lucky to live in a suburb, where sounds of the country could be heard in the back yards. Householders were permitted to keep hens and a neighbour across the road did just that, for the duration of the war. Some of the other neighbours registered with her instead of with the local grocer for the supply of eggs and we all helped her feed the hens by saving every leftover scrap of food for them. The cockerel was as reliable as any alarm clock and his morning call brought a breath of the farm to Kings Park.

During school holidays I was able to take care of our garden during the day, while Father was at work, maybe not everyone's idea of the perfect way to spend a holiday. I never looked upon it as hard work. Father had done away with our long herbaceous border as soon as war was declared and our neighbour, who was not interested in gardening, "lent" us his border, adjacent to our own. So we had a garden and a half. We grew all kinds of vegetables where once we had grown flowers and even the small front garden had ornamental edgings of parsley and beetroot. In the back garden there were beetroot, beans and broccoli, cabbages, carrots and celery, leeks and lettuces, peas, parsnips and potatoes and all kinds of salad crops. Above all we grew onions and shallots.

Of all the items that were in short supply during the war, onions seemed to be the most widely missed. There was no real substitute for the good old onion. Its flavour could do such a lot to give a lift to a wartime diet that, when shoppers did manage to buy even one onion, they felt quite elated. Because of the German U-boat attacks on our merchant fleet and the need to use shipping capacity for the war effort, items like onions were seldom imported and as a result, when out of season, they became very scarce indeed. We harvested our crop carefully, and hung them up for winter use. We were very lucky to have them. I remember Mother answering the front door bell one day. An old lady stood there. We did not know her, but she knew that we grew onions and she had screwed up her courage to ring our bell and beg for just one onion to take home with her! Mother was happy to oblige and that old lady would surely enjoy her dinner that day.

During the summer term of 1941, my class had suffered the trauma of the "qualifying" examination for secondary school. As soon as the holidays came round, I and some friends decided to do something unusual, as a change from the grind of working for the exam. Four of us decided to raise some money for charity. To this end, we agreed to write and perform a play, of all things! Our intentions were good, but our script was quite dreadful, I am sure. However, we took it very seriously. It was meant to be a spine-chilling "whodunnit" but it ended up, not surprisingly, as a farce. Jean, Marian, Diana and I met by turn, in each other's houses, and the summer days flew by as we planned the plot, the costumes and the "script". We called our play "The Ghost in Galoshes". Diana was the narrator; I was the archly aristocratic Lady Amelia; Marian was Joseph the butler, a double dealing, shifty character with a monocle; and Jean was Sam, the heavy footed, loud-talking, baccy-chewing American private eye, in spite of whom the mystery was solved in the end.

The four of us had the temerity to go round houses in Kings Park (by prior arrangement), performing our masterpiece, with never a blush. We took a collection afterwards and Marian's mother acted as our treasurer. Looking back, I think we should have paid our audiences for watching us! Nevertheless a lot of fun was generated by our piece of far from deathless prose and in the dark days of 1941, anything at all that raised a smile was welcome. Diana, Marian, Jean and I had our reward when, at the end of that summer, we saw in the *Evening Times* an acknowledgement thanking the "Ghost in Galoshes" for the donation to charity. We did have some very happy holidays, in spite of Hitler.

11. G.I.s AND MUTTON PIES

"Excuse me, Ma'am! Would you mind telling us what you folks call these things?" Mother was doing her Saturday morning shopping in Mount Florida when she was hailed thus. Standing firmly in her path were two American soldiers. Both were munching, with obvious relish, what Mother instantly recognised as Scotch mutton pies. Moreover, one of the soldiers was clutching a paper bag that bulged with further supplies. They must have bought about a dozen pies to eat between them. Mother answered their question, adding that they were sometimes referred to simply as "twopenny pies". Apparently the G.I.s wanted to know, so that they could ask for them by name in future. "They sure are good!" one said. Both declared they had never seen anything quite like our mutton pies before. The USA, as it seemed, with all its technology, produced nothing of the kind.

Mother had taken an instant liking to the Americans and they seemed to find in her an echo of their own mothers, whom they had left behind some months earlier when America had come into the war. It turned out that their names were Jack and Felix and they were part of a contingent of G.I.s who had just arrived in Britain.

They were based in Mount Florida School and that morning it looked as if every man in the contingent was out shopping in Cathcart Road. Mount Florida had seen nothing like that day in 1942.

Gallantry personified, Felix insisted on carrying Mother's shopping bag while she visited the various shops. Jack carried the bag of mutton pies, which was growing thinner and lighter as pie after pie was consumed.

Politely, they offered Mother one but, politely, she declined. Mother would not have been seen dead eating a pie in the street! There were some things she simply would not do, even at the risk of offending our American allies.

Jack and Felix had to turn down Mother's invitation to visit us at home, as they had to report back to the School at noon. They were leaving for an unknown destination and they were forbidden to write home to America until further notice. Both lads asked Mother if she would do them a great favour. They begged her to write to their mothers and say she had seen Jack and Felix and that they were well and happy. Of course Mother was only too pleased to do this and when she returned from her shopping trip to Mount Florida that day, she was fully equipped with writing pad and envelopes of air-mail stationery and the names and addresses of two ladies whom she had never met and would never visit.

As good as her word, Mother wrote to the mothers of Jack and Felix. I cannot say what she wrote, but I am sure it was everything that the American mothers wanted to know about their boys. In due course, the postman brought Mother a number of letters with strange postmarks. Not only had the American soldiers' mothers replied, but their sisters too had written to my mother. She was quite overwhelmed. But, as soon as time permitted, she filled her fountain pen and wrote, not two letters, this time, but four! The correspondence, which was started by a chance meeting and a mutton pie, lasted for many years and only petered out when Mother's arthritis made it too difficult for her to write legibly.

What really vexed Mother was being unable to send to America any up-to-date snapshots of our family. We had none to send. During the war, cameras were laid away in drawers and cupboards, because film was totally unobtainable for civilian use. This was a very sore point with me because my parents had given me a Kodak 620 Brownie camera for my tenth birthday, just before war broke out and I had not taken the chance to use it. Felix's sister sent a lot of snaps of their family and these were treasured by my mother.

Twice during the war, Jack's mother sent us parcels containing tins of ground coffee, tins of very sweet and sticky melon jam, packets of American sweets, chewing gum and several cotton tea towels. She had read with indignation that the people of Britain had to surrender precious clothing coupons for items of household linen and she felt this to be most unfair! Mother was touched by these kindly gestures but was in some difficulty over how best to reciprocate. So much was rationed here, or was in very short supply. She hit on the idea of sending something tartan, for did not all Americans love Scottish plaids? Her mind made up, off she went to the Argyle Arcade, in Buchanan Street, where she bought an authentic tartan tea cosy, with a sprig of white heather embroidered on one side. This, she reasoned, being unbreakable and light in weight, should travel the Atlantic without damage, U-boats permitting. She was right. Jack's coffee-drinking mother duly received the tartan tea cosy. I wish I had been there to see her open that parcel. I doubt if she had ever seen a tea cosy in her life before, and quite plainly she did not recognise this padded tartan object, elaborately trimmed with frills and embroidery. What on earth could it be? She must have made up her mind, to her own satisfaction if not to my mother's for, in due course, Mother received a charming letter from Jack's mother, thanking her for the "cute hankie sachet"!

After that, Mother had to choose her gifts for her American friends with all the care of a diplomat. She eventually took the easy way out and concentrated her gifts on the children, for by this time, she had learned that the sisters of both Jack and Felix had young families.

Recalling that my sister and I had always enjoyed children's annuals when we were small, one Christmas Mother bought the annual that featured Teddy Tail of the *Daily Mail*. Hopefully, she sent this off to America, praying that she had chosen wisely on this occasion. Her worries were groundless. The letters that came back to her were not merely polite acknowledgements. They were positively bubbling over with genuine enthusiasm. Teddy Tail, apparently, was as new and enjoyable to those American children as Scotch mutton pies had been to their uncle. In that American household, "Teddy Tail" became prescribed bedtime reading until the well-thumbed annual almost fell apart. Needless to say, Mother's Christmas gift problem was solved for several years to come and future editions of *Teddy Tail Annual* were carried proudly to school and shown off to American boys and girls as "A present from Mom's friend in England"!

12. STRANGE TO RELATE

Sometimes my daughters exchange a knowing look. They smile at me indulgently and not a word is spoken. I can read the message in their faces. Roughly translated, it says, "Poor Mum! She can't help it. She's not quite right in the head!" I see the look when I have given perfectly honest answers to some of their perpetual questions about what life was like at home during the war. Thirty-five years on, truth can sound remarkably like fiction, especially when I mention odd things, like gas buses and ladies with painted legs. The fact is that in wartime, we accepted as normal things that would have seemed strange in times of peace.

We knew that our white bread was not white. So what? We called it "white" because it was the whitest bread available. We got used to it. So much so, that the first truly white loaf that Mother brought home after the war caused a sensation in our house. We all just stared at it in disbelief! Placed alongside the last of the wartime white bread, it resembled an advertisement for Persil.

Bread was not alone in having a wartime guise. Tinned goods took on a strange new look. Gone was the shiny, see-your-face-in-it tin that we knew in peacetime. In its place was a bronzy brown metal, scarcely recognisable as tin. And goods that were habitually packed in tins began to appear in paper packets, where appropriate. Cocoa powder, for example, was largely sold in a packet, for decanting into an empty tin at home. It almost goes without saying that the empty packet, when discarded, was put in the wastepaper sack for reprocessing.

Decorated crockery became unobtainable. Cups, saucers and plates were starkly white and plain and had to rely on shape for a touch of individuality. Painted china took on a scarcity value and became a treasured luxury, while odd remnants of pre-war tea-sets fetched remarkably good prices at jumble sales.

Books that were printed in wartime, usually on inferior paper, bore the legend, "This book is produced in complete conformity with the authorised economy standards." They carried a motif made up of a lion couchant on top of an open book, bearing the words "Book Production War Economy Standard". Of course, we regretted the loss of high quality editions, but it was the words that mattered, not their presentation. Economy standard books were better than none at all.

Our school pencils, once clothed in brightly coloured coats of paint, suddenly appeared in naked wood, impressed with the legend "War Drawing". Our garden railings, once clothed in sober dark green paint, suddenly disappeared, sacrificed for the sake of the "war effort". We children of the neighbourhood watched acetylene welders perform this operation, our excitement mounting at first, then waning as we grew accustomed to the sight, just as we seemed to get used to all else that was unusual. After a few days, we would walk on without a second glance at the flying sparks…

Clothes rationing, introduced in 1941, gave rise to some quite bizarre economies, which we accepted without question because the reasons for them were clearly understood. My own children accuse me of pulling their legs today when I tell them about women painting their legs in wartime! It is perfectly true that some women did resort to painting their legs when they had no coupons to spare for stockings. "Were they Picts?" I am asked. Of course they were not, and the paint was not blue, although their cold legs might have been, underneath the coating of colour. The most popular shade of leg paint looked like suntan and, with practice, a smooth even coat could be applied, giving a finished appearance closely resembling a silk stocking. Sad to say, perfection was not always achieved and, in such cases, where the paint had run, or had gone on in blotches, the illusion was destroyed. At that time, women wore stockings with seams up the back. Care had to be taken to keep the seam straight because a crooked seam looked unsightly. As stocking seams were considered to give the legs a slimmer look, it was not surprising that the painters of imitation stockings also tried to emulate their silk or rayon prototypes, by drawing a thin dark line with eyebrow pencil or something similar, up the back of each leg. To keep the line straight – and thereby perform the feat of perfect legs – was no small achievement. I never tried it myself and I always admired the steady hand and skill of those who managed the job successfully.

The "Utility mark" entered our lives, emphasising usefulness and function and cutting out superfluous and wasteful trimmings. Not a square inch more material than was absolutely necessary could be used in manufacturing everyday products for home consumption, whether it was cardigans or carpets, bed-jackets or beds. Couples who married and set up house during the war found only a limited selection of furnishings available to them, in the "Utility range". The famous mark, made up of two capital Cs and the figure 41, was stamped or tagged on every item, from towels to tallboys. "Utility model" became an accepted expression in our vocabulary and was sometimes applied in ways never intended by its creators. When one young couple whom we knew had an addition to their family, the father, on being asked whether the baby was a boy or a girl, replied, "We got the utility model"! Women's lib was as yet unheard of!

For me, one unforgettable sight of wartime childhood was the gas buses. The first time I saw one, I thought it was a normal bus towing a dustbin on a trailer! An odd sight indeed and one that I lost no time in reporting to my father, who understood at once what I must have seen. He told me there had been buses fuelled by gas during the Great War. It was a means of saving petrol or diesel oil. The bus that I had seen had been converted to run on gas from the cylinder at the back. One of our local bus routes, the 4A as it was known then, now the 34, was selected as being suitable for conversion and the gas bus became a regular sight in Kings Park, as the 4A bus ran quite a frequent service. Unfortunately, the 4A bus also became quite a frequent sight, abandoned and alone, stuck about halfway up the steep hill on Menock Road. Gas seemed to lack the essential "oomph" of the more conventional fuels. Nevertheless, gas buses operated in Glasgow for a number of years. Personally, I was frightened of them and I disliked their smell. I was assured that they were perfectly safe and I have to admit that I never heard of one exploding or going on fire, but I had – and still have – a built-in distrust of gas of any kind. Perhaps Grandma's stories are to blame!

If the Public Transport Department saved fuel oil by using gas, then the Cleansing Department economised by using genuine horse power. We had the return of the horse and cart. As soon as we heard the familiar "clip-clop" of the big Clydesdale's hooves in the back lane, my sister and I used to rush down to the back garden gate with half an apple each, for Tommy, the cart-horse. So accustomed was he to being fed at our garden gate during school holidays that, on his first visit after we had gone back to school, Tommy was wont to search around for a substitute titbit. Once, he disgraced himself by taking a large bite out of Father's close-cropped privet hedge. It took years for Tommy's mark to grow out!

Perhaps the thought is unworthy, but, looking back, I wonder if Mother's gesture of kindness in feeding the horse was motivated solely by goodwill for Tommy? After munching his titbit, he had a habit of leaving his visiting card on the back lane, precisely at our garden gate, whence it could be swiftly scooped up on a shovel and added to our compost heap. There was much competition among neighbouring garden-lovers for such a prize!

In contrast to Tommy, the Clydesdale, was the pony of the briquette man. Compared with the Cleansing Department's cart, his rubber-tyred float was like a Rolls Royce. We seldom heard his approach and he had to depend on his shout of "Briquettes!" to bring us out to buy. We always did buy a dozen or two, because they were very cheap and they helped to stretch the coal allocation. One briquette placed on a red fire and banked up with dross could burn with a steady heat for a whole evening. If we had a lot of fine dross in the coal cellar, my father sometimes made his own version of a briquette, mixing the coal dust with cement and shaping it in a flower pot, like sand castles. But these lacked the fine texture of the commercial briquette. I wonder if there are such things obtainable nowadays. My children, brought up in the Scottish Highlands, had never heard of them until I told them about the briquette man and his pony.

My thoroughly modern daughters would have laughed if they had seen our ice-cream man. He was a regular visitor to our back lane in the summertime, for there were children in nearly every house in our road. No horse or pony for him! He got over the petrol problem by pedalling a converted tricycle. This carried a large refrigerated container and, when it was empty, he simply went back to base for a refill. His approach on rubber tyres was even quieter than the briquette man's and shrill blasts on a whistle were his signature tune, every bit as effective as the electronic chimes of today.

Horses and carts, briquettes and gas buses, to say nothing of the through traffic of tanks on trial in the Avenue, were all sights that were commonplace to us children of wartime Glasgow. Today, any one of them would make my children stare. I can understand why they give me odd looks when I talk about these things. And yet, I scarcely noticed them when they were there! I think I only began to take notice of some of them when they were, suddenly, not there anymore! It was the same with the fire buckets, which stood in pairs, one full of water, one full of sand, on every stair landing and corridor in public buildings. One automatically avoided them as one passed. I found myself continuing to avoid them for days after they had been removed, at the end of the war! Habit dies hard.

13. THE WIRELESS AND THE WAR

At home, we called our radio a wireless set. It had valves, not transistors and was in two quite separate parts, the receiver and the loudspeaker. It was a Cossor set, lovingly built in 1934 by that man of many skills, my Uncle John. How many stations it could receive I do not know. During the war, it was tuned to either the Home Service or the Forces Programme. Just occasionally, for a laugh, we twiddled the knobs until we found "Lord Haw-Haw", the German propagandist. After dark we seldom went out and we seemed to listen to the wireless a great deal.

I say "we" because the wireless set was in the living room and the four members of our family normally spent the evenings there, all together in the warmth from the only fire in our house. Anyone who wished solitude or peace and quiet faced the ordeal of an unheated room. The sitting room was used only when we had guests and the fire there was lit only when visitors were expected. At all other times unexpected callers found the warmth of their welcome cooled by the chilly surroundings. The bedrooms were similarly cold, a small gas fire being lit for just a short time in each room, while we were getting ready for bed. The bathroom was unspeakably chilly. Even to think about it brings me out in goose pimples. Because the water pipes in our house seemed especially vulnerable to frost, Mother kept a paraffin heater burning in the bathroom in cold weather. It was one of those very low heaters, designed for use under car engines and behind its protective wire mesh there burned a single flame, no bigger than that of a candle. Neither was its meagre heat very much more than that of a candle, but it was enough to keep the room temperatures above freezing, thereby protecting the pipes. The paraffin in the heater gave off a horrid smell and that was the first thing to greet me when I stepped into the house after school on winter afternoons.

How different it is today, when central heating is commonplace. My children linger long in the bath because of the comfortable warmth from radiator and heated towel rail, which they take for granted. For me at their age, such luxuries were considered to be confined to the USA! There was no likelihood of my lolling at length in a deep warm bath for two reasons. First, the temperature of the white tiled bathroom did not encourage loitering and second, the people of Britain were honour bound not to have their bath water more than four inches deep! This was part of the national economy drive to save energy and the nation had been informed that, by order of His Majesty King George V1, every bath in the royal household had been painted with a line denoting the permitted depth of water! Who was I, not to follow such an illustrious example?

All things considered, the living room was the most comfortable room in our house, warm and homely. Heavy chenille curtains shut out the draughts from the window and Mother kept a stuffed, sausage-shaped cushion on the floor at the door, to exclude the draught that in winter whistled mercilessly from the cold hall. Whenever one of us had to leave the room, to put the kettle on, or to visit the toilet, the door of the living room would be no sooner opened than the room temperature would plummet. What Grandma would have called "a stepmother's breath" would gush in, causing the door to be hastily closed and the sausage to be replaced with alacrity. Little wonder that the whole family spent nearly all its spare time round the fire in the warm living room. My sister and I both did our homework there, on either side of the dining table, under the centre light. My father relaxed in his armchair to the left of the fireplace, reading and sometimes dozing and Mother had a similar armchair to the right of the hearth. Her workbox stood beside her and always she seemed to be busy knitting or sewing.

The hearth had three tiles missing for most of the war years. They had broken with fierce heat of the fire and, because the builders, MacTaggart and Mickel, had imported the tiles from Germany in 1929, we were quite unable to find matching replacements during the war. No English pottery could be found that produced tiles of that precise shape and colour. I remember the colour was "teapot brown". Neither shall I ever forget the number of tiles round the arch of the fire. A strange memory, perhaps? There were seventeen, to begin with and latterly, fourteen tiles and three gaps. I wish I had a pound for every time I counted them. I should be rich today. In times of stress, when one is upset or worried, it can help to calm the nerves if one deliberately concentrates very hard on something unrelated to the cause of the distress. My remedy, on such occasions, as I sat in the semi-circle at the fire, was to count the tiles over and over again, until I regained a grip on myself. I always felt shy about crying in public, even in the presence of my family. And during the war, there was a limit to the extent to which even a child could be sheltered from the cruel realities of war.

The wireless set brought the war and its sadness to our own fireside every night, without fail, for the BBC *9 O'Clock News* was compulsive listening in our house, as in most others. Eye witness reports from BBC correspondents on the spot did much to bring vivid reality to the news. Richard Dimbleby, Frank Gillard, Edward Ward and Godfrey Talbot were just a few of these brave men. Often, a talk on current affairs would follow the evening bulletin and these talks were usually so interesting that, even at my age, I listened with close attention. Among the speakers, I remember J.B. Priestley and a promising young RAF officer, called Squadron Leader John Strachey. One such talk haunted me for a long time afterwards and caused me to count those hearth tiles repeatedly. It was a graphic description given by a seaman who had survived after his ship had been broken in two on being torpedoed while in convoy. The appalling suffering that he endured, literally going through fire and water before his rescue, froze me with horror. It left me – and all who heard that broadcast, I feel sure – with a much clearer understanding of what the Battle of the Atlantic really meant to us all.

A regular speaker after the *9 O'Clock News* on Sundays was the "Radio Padre", the Rev. Ronald Selby-Wright. A gifted broadcaster, his weekly chats were easy to listen to and time passed so quickly during his talks that one scarcely felt that fifteen minutes had flown by. He must have been a comfort and inspiration to millions of listeners over the years. One of his talks was almost due to be broadcast when he received news that Jimmie, one of "his boys", from the Canongate Boys' Club, which he ran in Edinburgh, had been killed in action. Scrapping his prepared script, the Radio Padre came on the air that evening and talked from his heart about the one thing that was uppermost in his mind at that moment, the grievous loss of Jimmie. In earlier broadcasts and in published books, Mr. Selby-Wright had often spoken of his boys' club and their sports champion, Jimmie. Like many another lad, Jimmie had been called up for National Service and now, like many another lad, he had laid down his life. The Padre had lost a loved one and, because his listeners felt that, through the radio talks, they too knew Jimmie, they shared his loss. That evening's broadcast was one of the most poignant I have ever heard. No commissioned officer ever received a more moving valedictory than did Jimmie – Private James Dalgleish – when, in the words of the Padre, "the trumpets sounded for him on the other side". For me, held firmly in the grip of the radio padre's words, it was quite useless to count the tiles on the hearth. The tears were coursing down my cheeks and I was not ashamed.

Although there was much on the wireless that made compelling listening, I never experienced any difficulty in closing my ears to the sound around me if I had homework to do, or an engrossing book to read. So it was one evening, towards the end of May, 1941. I was busy with some homework, because, for me, it was the year of the dreaded Qualifying Examination. The *9 O'Clock News* started as usual with the wartime ritual of the announcer stating his name. I paid no attention to what he was saying until my mother let out a gasp of horror, which suggested an unwillingness to believe what she had just heard. "The Hood!" "The Hood" – *H.M.S. Hood* – had been lost with all hands, blown to smithereens by a shot in one of her magazines from the German battleship *Bismarck*. To us, that meant that David, the boy next door, was dead.

It was like a death in the family. David's father was a manager in the S.C.W.S factory at Shieldhall and Mother, until her marriage, had been on his staff. She had known the family for many years and had watched David and his sister grow up. David had regarded Mother as a kind of Auntie and, for her part, I think that Mother looked upon David as the son she never had. He used to tell her about all his outdoor adventures, first with the Scouts and latterly with the Rovers. He was a keen climber and the house next door was habitually swarming with David's friends, either planning their next weekend climb or tinkering with David's latest acquisition, his motor bicycle.

When he was called up for National Service, David chose to serve in the Royal Navy. On what was to prove to be his last home leave, he came in to see us on the evening before his departure, in full Seaman's uniform. We never stood on ceremony with David and he was ushered, not into the cold splendour of the sitting room, but into the bosom of the family, round the fire in the living room. As usual, I felt shy and awkward and said very little. I remember that David stayed for quite a while, chatting to my parents, but I was conscious of an element of strain, unusual in the presence of one so happy-go-lucky as he was. Mother was never good at saying "goodbye" and, in wartime, one could never be certain that the parting would only be temporary. I suspect that it came as a relief to all concerned when David's visit that evening came to an end. I am sure that Mother felt instinctively that she would not see David again for a long time, but she could not possibly have foreseen that none of us would ever see him again.

Within a few weeks of David's visit, *H.M.S. Hood* and all her crew were lost.

It says a lot for how up to date the BBC news bulletins were that we should hear of the sinking of the "Hood" on the *9 O'Clock News*, before David's father had received the dreaded official telegram intimating his son's death in action.

It was said that Mr Churchill did not like speaking on the radio but, from time to time, the Prime Minister found it necessary to broadcast to the nation. His talks usually followed the evening news bulletins and commanded close attention throughout Britain. I think I must have heard them all. I certainly remember some of his characteristic phrases, which although I did not realise it at the time, were to go down in history and become part of the Churchill legend. "Blood, toil, tears and sweat", "Give us the tools and we will finish the job", and "Some chicken, some neck!" made good rousing listening and I am sure they revived the flagging spirit of the British public at times when such a boost to the morale was vital to the nation's war effort. British and proud of it, Mr Churchill obstinately declined to give the word "Nazi" its German pronunciation. He invariably spat it out, pronouncing it as if it were an English word spelt "nazzy". A small gesture, but we loved to hear him do it. It was as if he were thumbing his nose at Adolf Hitler.

The part played by the BBC during the war, bringing news, entertainment and, on occasion, leadership and inspiration to the people of the free world cannot be measured. I remember the broadcast that launched the famous "Victory V" all over Europe. Listeners were shown how to tap the Morse "V" – dot, dot, dot, dash – signifying the syllables in the phrase "Victory V". They were encouraged to play the opening bars of Beethoven's Fifth Symphony, which beat the same rhythm. They were asked to use their fingers to show the "V" sign, which became one of the Prime Minister's favourite gestures. All this at a time when the German armies had overrun Europe. The BBC transmissions, in spite of being officially banned in occupied countries, got through to the underground resistance workers and they took up the "V" sign and rhythm, to the torment of the invaders. The snowball begun by that broadcast was to become an avalanche.

Every Christmas, the King's broadcast to his people had an audience of many millions. I looked upon him as a father figure, with two daughters much of an age with my sister and me, evacuated to Windsor, while he and the Queen remained in London, sharing with their people the dangers of bombing that the capital city always faced. One Christmas Day very early in the war – I think it was 1939 – the King concluded his message with a quotation. I was never good at memorising prose but there was a quality in those lines that appealed strongly to me and I had no difficulty in recalling them, on many future occasions. The words of inspiration that His Majesty commended to his people at the beginning of another year of war were:

I said to the man who stood at the Gate of the Year,
"Give me a light, that I may tread safely into the unknown."
And he replied, "Go out into the darkness and put your hand into the Hand of God.
That will be to you better than light and safer than a
known way."

14. ON THE LIGHTER SIDE

Although news, views, prayers and patriotism figured prominently in the BBC's wartime schedule, the light entertainment programmes were no less important. Hitler had hoped to break the morale of the British people and his failure to do so was in some measure due to the BBC. It's programmes reached out to isolated out-posts and brought music to soothe or stimulate, plays and stories to divert our thoughts and comedy to help us laugh at the hardships that war had imposed upon us.

To avoid having all its eggs in one basket, the BBC was evacuated, at least in part, from London to "somewhere in England". I suppose that they must have operated, in the very early days of the war, with a skeleton staff. Certainly, the same cast lists and permutations and combinations of the names on the lists kept cropping up. The BBC Repertory Company seemed to consist of a handful of talented Jacks and Jills of all trades who gave the impression of being available for live transmissions at a moment's notice. I cannot imagine what the BBC would have done without the Trojan service it received from troupers like C. Denier Warren, Betty Huntly-Wright, Dudley Rolph, Clarence Wright, Gladys Young,

Marjorie Westbury, James MacKechnie and others like them. They seemed to be able and willing to turn their hand to anything. Another stalwart who seemed to carry the BBC on his shoulders at that time was the never to be forgotten Sandy MacPherson, the BBC organist. Whenever a gap in the programme schedule occurred, Sandy seemed to be on hand to fill it with organ music of all kinds. He initiated request programmes. Heart-rending radio links were forged between evacuee children and their parents, and between Service personnel and their folk at home. Mother used to shed tears every time she heard these programmes, but she would not miss them, for all that. Personally, at my age, they made me squirm with embarrassment!

On weekday mornings, I used to time my own personal schedule by the programmes on the wireless. *Lift up your Hearts*, a five minute religious programme before the news, signalled time for me to get out of bed. The end of the *8 O'Clock News* meant I should be washed and dressed and *On the Kitchen Front* or *The Radio Doctor*, both five minute spots after the news bulletin, meant that I should be starting breakfast.

Then I was off to school until lunchtime. On week days between 12.30pm and 1.00pm, the BBC broadcast a variety programme aimed at factory workers' lunch break. It was introduced by Bill Gates and was called *Workers' Playtime*. Personally, I thought it quite diabolical, but mine was the harsh, unsympathetic judgement of a child. *Workers' Playtime* attracted some of the big names in show business, like Mr Gillie Potter, Suzette Tarri, and Jeanne de Casalis, and it must have been a popular programme to last all those years. When the *1 O'Clock News* ended, it was time for me to re-pack my school bag and return for afternoon classes.

Home again about 4.30pm, my first aim was not to listen but to eat! Blackcurrant purée was a passable substitute for jam though lacking in sweetness, and I used to spread it directly on a slice of bread without butter or margarine, because there was very little butter in the week's ration and I detested wartime margarine. Hunger satisfied, the wireless would be plugged in for *Children's Hour* at 5.00pm.

The standard of BBC radio programmes for children then was as high as it is for TV children's programmes today. Under the friendly guidance of Kathleen, Doris and Muriel, Elizabeth, David and Uncle Mac, my sister and I – and Mother, too – really enjoyed a wide variety of items – songs and poems, adventure stories, serialised plays, quiz programmes and even current affairs. Vernon Bartlett and Stephen King-Hall were among my favourite speakers. And there were outdoor programmes with Romany and The Hut Man, when we learned a lot about country life, quite painlessly. Of course, it is true that one cannot please all of the people all of the time. My friend Jean simply could not bear to listen to one particular series of programmes, broadcast from Scotland. Supposed to depict a gathering of a farmer and his family, their farm worker and their neighbours, for a musical entertainment and a cup of tea in the farm kitchen, it was called *Down at the Mains* Jean renamed it "Down at the Drains"! 'Nough said!

Children's Hour was followed by the news at 6 o'clock, when we were usually busily engaged in preparations for the evening meal and Father's return from work. After the dishes were washed and put away, we would all get on with our own individual pursuits. Father would probably do some gardening if the evening light permitted, Mother would sit down with her sewing and my sister and I would work steadily through our homework. There always seemed to be plenty of that. To allow us to have peace and quiet to concentrate on our lessons, the wireless was not usually plugged in, on weekdays, before nine o'clock when the evening news commanded attention.

There was one exception. "ITMA!" That comedy half-hour, at 8.30pm, (on Thursdays I think) must have been one of the most sensational successes in the history of the BBC. Its full title was *It's That Man Again* but this was soon abbreviated to its initials and the programme became known as *ITMA*. Its fast talking star was the late Tommy Handley and among others that I remember in the cast over the years until Tommy's untimely death were Jack Train, Horace Percival, Dorothy Summers, Sidney Keith, Doris Nicholls, Hattie Jacques, Clarence Wright, Molly Weir and Sam Costa.

The show had a galaxy of bizarre characters who popped up every week and catch phrases soon abounded. A few that spring to mind are:

"The Diver" – "Don't forget the diver, sir! Don't forget the diver!"

"The Commercial Traveller" – "Good morning! Nice day!"

"Mrs Mopp" – "Can I do you now, sir?" and "Ta-ta for now!" (Later T.T.F.N.)

"Claude and Cecil" – "After you, Claude! No! After you, Cecil!"

And, of course, there was my favourite character, the German spy called "Funf". He was played by the late Jack Train, with a heavy German accent, made to sound sinister and sepulchral by means of speaking into a glass tumbler. Here was a spy cast in the genuine mould of *The Dandy* or *The Beano*! I adored the elusive Funf and his catch phrase, "This is Funf speaking!"

The *ITMA* catch phrases took Britain by storm and they could be heard in schools, factories, offices, bus-queues, in fact, wherever a situation seemed to suit a particular catch phrase. Even dignified business men were known to quote "After you, Claude!" when ushering clients into their offices. "T.T.F.N." almost replaced "Goodbye" or "Cheerio" at our school. *ITMA* was quite unique and a wonderful tonic for its listeners over the years. It was a stunning shock to his millions of fans when Tommy Handley died very suddenly.

Of course, there were other radio shows, which brightened the darkness of wartime. Some were aimed at a particular branch of the Services, like *Navy Mixture*, with Doris Hare. Occasionally, we were introduced to promising talent from the Services, like a young singer in the R.C.A.F., called Ted Hockridge. I can also remember a ten year old girl making her radio début, singing to the troops. Her name was Petula Clark.

Vera Lynn's star rose in wartime and has never set. She was known, deservedly, as "The Forces' Sweetheart" and her charm came over the air to touch the hearts of her audiences everywhere. Mother never could suffer "crooners", but Vera changed all that. Mother loved her!

Nowadays, music-hall seems almost to have perished as a recognised form of entertainment, but John Sharman produced an hour-long show for the BBC every Saturday night, for many years. I am sure it ran all during the war, with only short breaks between each series. It was called, simply, *Music Hall* and was broadcast from 8pm until 9pm. Just about every big name in show business appeared in that show, I should think. I remember Nellie Wallace, George Robey, Flotsam and Jetsam, the Hulberts, the Western

Brothers, "Hutch", the Two Leslies, Wee Georgie Wood, Sandy Powell, Stainless Stephen, Flanagan and Allen, Gwen Catley, Helen Hill and countless others.

Music Hall was followed by the inevitable news bulletin at nine o'clock and then by *Saturday Night Theatre*. For our family, this programme was the radio highlight of the week. The standard of acting was consistently high and the range of plays was wide and varied. I was allowed to stay up late on Saturdays to listen and, thanks to the BBC, I received in this delightfully enjoyable way and excellent introduction to a variety of plays by many authors. They ranged from J.M. Barrie to H.G. Wells, from Ibsen to Euripides, from fantasy, mystery and farce, to Greek and Shakespearean tragedy. We were absorbed in the spoken word, never for a moment missing the visual element now provided by television. The war was temporarily forgotten.

Quiz programmes were another popular feature of wartime broadcasting and they inspired impromptu imitation, helping to pass weary hours in places where the only entertainment was of the do-it-yourself variety. The earliest type of quiz that I can remember was the straightforward spelling bee, full of "hardy annuals" like "antirrhinum". Gradually, the range of questions widened, to cover music, literature and general knowledge. Some quiz programmes were clearly enjoyed as much by the participants as by the listeners. Tongue-twisters were always great fun and, if they were difficult to rhyme off at speed with a straight face, they were well-nigh impossible when the contestant was tied in knots with laughter. Some of the actual tongue-twisters used in these programmes were already familiar to me, because they were in use at school for hand-writing practice, e.g. "Round and round the rugged rocks the ragged rascals ran." But I learned many new ones, some being more twisted than others! The two that never failed to twist my tongue were "The Leith police dismisseth us," and "Are you aluminiuming, my man?" "No, I'm copper-bottoming, ma'am." Try those at speed, six times over!

The wartime years were during the era of the "big bands" and my sister and I listened as keenly to their broadcasts as today's teen-agers listen to their favourite pop groups. The selection of bands that were on the air regularly was quite staggering, by today's stand-ards. We had our favourite bands and singers, of course, but we did not discriminate against any. I think we listened for the sake of the tunes that were played and sung rather than for the merit of the actual orchestra. Mother's favourite was Henry Hall and his Orchestra, and she liked Bruce Trent and Georgina, who were among his singers. My sister liked Billy Cotton's Band, with Alan Breeze, and also Joe Loss and his Orchestra. I think my favourite was Geraldo and his Orchestra, with Len Camber, Dorothy Carless, George Evans and Jackie Hunter.

The song writers were kept busy churning out material, and although many wartime songs were short-lived, some have lingered in my memory, like "Amapola (Pretty Little Poppy)", "Lili Marlene", and "We'll Meet Again". There were nonsense songs, to make us smile, like "Three Little Fishes" and "Mares Eat Oats". One song began "Casey would dance with the strawberry blonde, and the band played on". That was just what the big bands did throughout the war, bombs or no bombs. And, in the very act of playing on, some paid with their lives. We heard with sadness, of the deaths of singer Al Bowley and band leader Ken "Snakehips" Johnson, during bombing raids. They died because, in their code of practice, the show must go on. The fight to keep up the morale of the people was as important a battle as any fought with guns, and the part played by entertainers in winning that fight should never be undervalued.

15. LENDING A HAND

Normally, girls who join a Brownie pack progress to a Guide company. In my own case, I reversed the procedure. This is how it happened.

The highlight of the year in Guiding, was the summer camp. Because I had a history of kidney trouble, sitting or lying on cold, possibly damp, ground was forbidden to me and camping was out of the question. Denied that, I could see little to attract me to the Guide movement. My two closest friends, Jean and Marian, had joined one of the local Guide companies when they were eleven, and quite dispassionately, I had watched them progress from the Tenderfoot stage, through enrolment, to gain their first few badges and become patrol leaders. Frankly, it all left me rather cold. I had never been a Brownie and I guessed that I could never be a Guide. It was strange that I should feel like that, in view of the fact that Jean, Marian and I were such close friends and had such a lot in common with each other. In school, the staff referred to us as "The Three Musketeers". Mother found this out one Parents' Day, when our form teacher told her that it was the talk of the staffroom how three girls who were the keenest rivals where school work was concerned could be such inseparable friends. Certainly, we seemed to go everywhere and do everything together – with the exception of joining the Guides.

My change of heart occurred when I heard that Brown Owl, the lady who was in charge of the Brownie pack, was in need of two Pack leaders. Her former helper, Tawny Owl, had been called up for the Women's Services and Brown Owl was looking for younger girls to help her, to ensure that they, too, would not be whisked away to the army in a short time. That was the trouble with training sixteen- and seventeen-year-olds for youth work in wartime. No sooner were they trained and just beginning to be of real use, than they were called up.

I was interested in Brown Owl's predicament. In the school play-ground, I often talked to the primary school children and I felt at ease in their company. With them, I did not feel shy and I could be my natural self. Could I, perhaps, help Brown Owl as a Pack leader? Jean pointed out the snag. Pack leaders were required to be enrolled Girl Guides! That did it. I was hooked! Without further hesitation, I reported to the Guide Captain that Wednesday evening, and was accepted as a new recruit. I was twelve, quite old to be starting at the beginning, but I had a target to aim for and I worked through my tests with all possible speed. At the earliest opportunity, I was enrolled as a Girl Guide and, that very same week, I reported for duty as a Pack leader with the Brownies. Jean had agreed to go with me and the two of us, from then on, went to Brownies on Tuesdays and Guides on Wednesdays.

I enjoyed working and playing with the Brownies as much as I had anticipated and in the Pack I found quite a few of my little playground friends. I had to admit, eventually, that I was enjoying the Guide meetings, too, in spite of my earlier disinterest. I rapidly completed my Second Class badge work and became a patrol leader like Jean and Marian. So the three of us had more in common than ever.

Guides and Brownies did not meet during the school holidays and, with the end of the school term, in June, came the final meetings of the Guide and Brownie session. In August, quite unexpectedly, I received a letter from Brown Owl. I read it, read it again, and dashed off to visit Jean. At the top of the hill, I met Jean, on her way to visit me! She, too, had received a letter from Brown Owl. The two letters were the same. Brown Owl was letting us know that, due to unforeseen circumstances, she had resigned her Warrant. Come September and the start of the new Brownie session, Jean and I would be in charge of our Pack. Brown Owl wished us luck! We were at that time barely thirteen years of age. Talk about being left to hold the baby? Some baby! A Pack of twenty four Brownies was quite a handful.

Nevertheless, Jean and I accepted our new and unexpected responsibility. What else could we do? Had we declined, the Pack would have been disbanded and, in turn, the Guide company would have lost its chief source of recruitment. The District Commissioner visited us on the evening of our first "solo" meeting and gave us plenty of encouragement. We were to be entrusted with the entire running of the Pack, except for the actual enrolment of recruits. This ceremony could be conducted only by a Warranted Guider. What we did was to invite our own Guide Captain and one of the Brown Owls from the other Packs in the neighbourhood to come along whenever we had recruits ready for enrolment.

Everything else – collecting subscriptions, paying bills, and banking the funds – was left to us to manage.

Brownie meetings began at 6.15pm and finished at 7.30pm, in time to let the children get to bed at a reasonable hour. Jean and I were seldom home before 8.30pm however, because we had to see the Brownies safely home. Nowadays, parents tend to collect their children in the family car. In wartime, the family car, if there was one, tended to be laid up for the "duration". There was no petrol for joyriding. Because of the blackout, we could not allow children of Brownie age to walk home unaccompanied, so Jean would take half the Pack and I would take the other half and off we would go, like a couple of pied pipers, the children following the beam of our torches. One by one, the Brownies would be safely delivered to their homes, all over Kings Park and Croftfoot, until, at the farthest points on our respective treks, Jean and I would find ourselves alone, with quite a long walk home. I used to enjoy these walks with the children. They chattered ceaselessly and the only squabbling that ever took place was over which two Brownies were to hold my hands on any particular evening. By comparison, my walk back home was very quiet.

In spite of our lack of a Warranted Guider, Jean and I allowed the Pack to participate to the full in any District or Division activities that were arranged. The first such project to arise after we were left in charge was a concert. I think it must have been a Divisional scheme, because the actual performance took place in a church hall in Newlands, quite a distance from Kings Park. With some trepidation, for we had no experience of such things, Jean and I agreed that our Pack's contribution to the concert programme should be an action-song version of "Ten Little Nigger Boys".* For this, we picked ten Brownies of approximately the same height. It might have been more conventional to have chosen the ten best singers but we had our reasons! In any case, every single child in our Pack seemed to be able to sing and did so at the slightest encouragement.

If ever there was a spare minute or two in the programme that Jean or I had drawn up for a particular Brownie meeting, we had no trouble filling the gap. We simply called out, "Who wants to do a party piece?", and we were besieged by volunteers. I, who was so shy, used to marvel at their total lack of self-consciousness. But I noticed that as those same children matured, in their later years, in the Guide company, they too went through a period of shyness and became almost self-effacing for a time. It was all part of the process of growing up, I expect.

We wanted ten girls of similar height because we were taking the easy way out where costumes were concerned. Partly because of clothes rationing and partly because of the distance that we had to travel, by public transport, to the actual concert, we wanted to use as few "props" as possible. We hit on the idea of having a line of washing hanging across the stage, from one side to the other. The

---

* A note from Sarah and Helen: The song Mum refers to in this chapter was, at the time of the Brownie performance, commonly sung in homes and schools across the Western world. This, in today's society, would be completely inappropriate. At the time, however, American Minstrel music was very popular and our grandpa probably entertained Mum and Auntie Helen by playing a repertoire of these on the family harmonium. Indeed, when we were children in the 1970s *The Black and White Minstrel Show* was on BBC1 as Saturday night entertainment. Thankfully our world has become much more tolerant and respectful. The song title has been adapted over the years, and has eventually become a song about ten little teddy bears, each meeting their own particular/peculiar fate. We have chosen to leave the wording of the chapter as Mum wrote it originally, as it reflects just how perplexing her era seemed to us as children. We mean to cause no offence.

clothes on the line were pegged closely together and consisted of big articles, like night dresses and bath towels, which reached to the ground, forming a colourful screen. The performers were lined up behind the "washing", only their heads showing above the line. Jean, concealed behind a stage curtain, held one end of the rope at shoulder height – Brownie shoulder height, of course – and I, similarly concealed, at the opposite side of the stage, held the other end of the rope and pulled it taut. It was easy enough to obtain ten scraps of brightly coloured material to conceal ten heads of hair, and cocoa powder and lipstick did the rest. Before that concert was over, I became quite expert at tying head squares in turban style! One by one, verse by verse, the ten Brownies bobbed down, out of sight behind the screen of washing, until, at the end of the song, all ten jumped up with a final shout.

The concert was a highly polished, well-rehearsed affair and was the big success that it deserved to be. Our own Pack did not disgrace themselves. Far from it. They enjoyed their own performance so much that their happiness fairly shone out of those ten, cocoa powdered faces. The audience loved them and, listening to the applause from our hiding places, Jean and I felt that, as Pack leaders, we had come through our baptism of fire, unscathed. That gave us the courage and desire to continue "holding the baby."

After that concert, Jean and I led the Pack in a number of quite ambitious projects, during the next few years. A picnic in the park, a pantomime in town, church parades and Brownie Revels, were some of these departures from the regular weekly Pack meetings.

Brownie Revels were a kind of grand scale District picnic, usually held on a Saturday afternoon in early summer. Every Pack in the District was invited to take part. If there were six Packs participating, a programme would be drawn up, consisting of six items, for example, a team game, a game played in a circle, a skipping rope game, a singing game, a story and last, but not least, a picnic meal. The organising Brown Owls would station themselves in different parts of the field and each would concentrate on her chosen item all afternoon. The Packs made a circuit of the organisers, moving on to the next station at pre-arranged intervals. At the end of the Revels, each Pack would have done everything on the programme once – and each long suffering organiser would have done her own item six times in succession. On one occasion, when it fell to me to be one of the organisers, I made a great mistake. I volunteered to tell a story. All might have gone well had the weather been fine on the Saturday afternoon of the Revels. We could all have spread out, keeping each Pack at a reasonable distance from its neighbours. But it rained without ceasing all that afternoon. We had to transfer the Revels to the school gymnasium, which was fairly big but, from my point of view, not big enough. My well-rehearsed story, timed to perfection, to meet the scheduled programme, was not so much told as bawled. Shouting a traditional fairy story six times in succession, with scarcely a break, is the quickest way I know to a very sore throat. The next day was Sunday and, in our house, it was even quieter than usual, for I was quite hoarse.

There were, I have to admit, some facets of my work with the Brownies that I endured rather than enjoyed. The monthly church parade came into this category. Our Pack, together with the Cubs, Scouts and Guides, was expected to attend the monthly Youth Service in the church whose hall we used and, as every Brownie on enrolment promised "To do her duty to God", that seemed only appropriate. For me, it was a double ordeal.

In the first place, the church was the local Episcopal Church and I, a Presbyterian, was not too familiar with the order of service. I worried about perhaps not knowing the psalm tunes and about the possibility of losing my way in the prayer book! In the second place, the Brownies always led the other youth organisations into the church and that meant occupying the two front rows – a very conspicuous position. There was one centre aisle, and the Pack leaders had to sit at the end of the rows, next to the aisle, open to the full gaze of the congregation. When we rose to our feet, I used to feel like a Goliath in the midst of rows of Davids. Experience taught me to swot up on the order of service and thereby put an end to my worries on that score. I also found it expedient to learn by heart the first few verses of a number of hymns. This was because, as soon as the rector announced the number of the hymn that we were about to sing, hymn books began to be passed along to me as though on a conveyor belt, for me to turn up the correct page. By the time I had performed this service for the last Brownie in the row, the congregation was usually starting on the third verse! To enable me to sing while I feverishly turned the pages in book after book, I found it helped to know the words by heart.

During the sermon, the Brownies invariably grew restless, writhing and wriggling, even although in the front two rows they were under the nose of the rector. He was good with children, and put much work into making his sermons intelligible to the young-sters at the church parade. But he could not stop the Brownies from fidgeting. (The Cubs were just as bad!) It was quite inevitable that at least one Brownie in the Pack would drop her collection coin. Far from landing on its side and lying quietly where it fell, as befitted its surroundings, the church collection penny always seemed to roll noisily away! Sometimes it would pirouette like a spinning top, before landing on its side with a chink that in the quietness of the church sounded to my burning ears like a stroke of Big Ben. If my arm stretched far enough, a swift grab at the back of the Brownie uniform belt was sufficient to restrain the bereft Brownie from diving under the seats in search of her lost coin. If the miscreant was beyond my reach, I could only try to look nonchalant, and pray that the bumps and shuffles from the far end of the front row were not as noticeable to others as they were to me.

Bumps and bruises were common enough in the rough and tumble of some of the more boisterous games that featured in an average weekly Brownie meeting. Jean and I had done a little First Aid in Guides but we seldom had occasion to practise it. The panacea for all minor ills and accidents was the "Brownie smile". Whenever tears appeared, or the corners of a mouth turned down, following a bump or a fall, happiness could be restored on the instant by asking the sufferer to remember her "Brownie smile". This was a special smile, which went "from ear to ear"! It was alleged to have a magical quality, in that when it was turned on, all who saw it felt that they wanted to smile, too. It never let me down. The magic really worked! Whenever I saw an erstwhile sad little face break forth into this big smile, I invariably beamed back – usually from relief that another small crisis had been averted!

As well as the Brownie smile, there were the Brownie promise, the Brownie law, the Brownie salute, the Brownie handshake and the Brownie motto – "Lend a Hand". One evening, when I was taking a Pack meeting, single-handed, the mother of one of the children arrived, to take her daughter home. She was early and I invited her to sit down and watch the latter part of the evening's programme. When she was on the point of leaving the hall with her daughter, that harassed mother told me she marvelled at how – at my age – I could keep control of a whole bunch of Brownies, when she – an adult – had difficulty in looking after just one. "Don't you ever wish there was something called "the Brownie slap?" she asked me!

I had occasion to recall her words when the war ended and demobilisation began. The fathers of most of our Brownies came marching home. Families long divided by war service were re-united. It was only natural that the fathers should compensate for previous deprivation of their children's company by spoiling them thoroughly, at least for a short while. The effect on the children's behaviour was immediately apparent. During their father's absence, their overworked mothers had kept a tight rein, sending the children to bed promptly and generally insisting on good manners and obedience. This had made life easy for Jean and me, because the good training at home was reflected in the behaviour of the children at Brownies. They were biddable and obedient. The change came quite abruptly. Suddenly, Jean and I found our words falling on deaf ears. Silence, previously obtained in a trice by a mere hand signal, became a scarce commodity. Discipline deteriorated. For the first time, I began to feel the strain. I even began to wish that there was such a thing as the Brownie slap! What had been easy when I was thirteen was proving to be hard work at seventeen.

I stuck it for a further seven years, during which I obtained first my Tawny Owl's Warrant and then my Brown Owl's Warrant. But, in the aftermath of the war, I began to feel that I was fighting a battle, to keep up the previous standards of the Pack and that is quite the wrong frame of mind in which to approach youth work.

It should not feel like a battle. I realised, eventually, that I was no longer enjoying working – and playing – with my little friends. I was tired – worn out, I suppose. It was time for me to go, before the children detected my feelings. I resigned my Warrant, after eleven years with the Pack. I felt as if I had spent a life time with the Brownies, although I was not yet twenty-four years old.

That was just one aspect of how the war affected my life. One cannot exempt oneself from war. However, insidiously, it reaches out and touches every living soul. Had the war not claimed Tawny Owl's services in 1942, I should never have given a thought to joining the Brownie movement at all. Had the war not forced a relaxation in rules, Jean and I should never have been allowed to run a Brownie pack at an age that, in peacetime, would be regarded as ridiculously young. Yet it all happened and Jean and I survived the experience. But, speaking for myself, I think it put years on me!

16. CHIPS AND CHAR

However small my contribution might be, I wanted to help win the war. My chance came after I joined the Girl Guides.

Their National Service Badge was awarded annually to all Guides who could produce evidence showing that, in the course of the year, they had put in a minimum of ninety-six hours of recognised service in aid of the war effort. My friend, Marian, who was a collector for her father's National Savings Group, had already earned her first year's badge. It was not like the normal Girl Guide badges for Proficiency, which were worn on the tunic sleeves. The National Service Badge consisted of a square of navy blue silky material with a crown embroidered in gold. This was stitched to the front of the tunic, above the pocket. Underneath, were stitched date strips, one for each year of approved National Service. Marian was the first Guide in our company to receive one of these badges and she was justly proud of it. It put the rest of us on our mettle. Somehow, somewhere, we simply had to find something useful to do. My friend Jean's Aunt Mary solved our problem.

Once a week, this lady did voluntary work in the Y.M.C.A. canteen, which was then at Eglinton Toll, in the south side of

Glasgow. She and a number of other ladies were on the Saturday afternoon shift, one of the busiest periods of all. Extra help was never refused and Jean went along to the canteen with her Aunt one afternoon to see what it was like and to lend a hand. The supervisor welcomed her warmly and put her to work at once! As she had expected, Jean discovered that working in the canteen was no picnic. That afternoon, she and the other volunteers toiled solidly for the three hours that the shift covered, and they did not even have time to snatch a cup of tea for themselves. Nevertheless, Jean enjoyed the experience. She did not mind the hard work for she was young and strong. She could tolerate missing her tea, for she knew that a meal would be waiting for her when she got home. What she did miss was company of her own age.

Her colleagues at the canteen were mostly contemporaries of her Aunt Mary and even the few younger ones were much older than Jean, who was after all only fourteen at that time. Girls, as well as boys, were called up for National Service at the age of eighteen and only those who had been granted exemption, for one reason or another, were available for voluntary work. So the canteen staff comprised of women who were too old for National Service or otherwise exempt from it.

The following Wednesday – Guide night – Jean treated her fellow patrol leaders to a graphic account of how she had spent Saturday afternoon at the Y.M.C.A. canteen. The result was that three of us – Mary, Gina and I – volunteered to keep Jean company at the canteen on future Saturdays. We reckoned that, in thirty-two weeks time, we could all complete ninety-six hours of canteen duty to qualify for the coveted National Service Badge! The more we discussed the idea, the keener we grew.

That night I arrived home from the Guide meeting all agog with the news of my big opportunity to do my bit for the war effort! Mother did not share my enthusiasm. Mother-like, she could find all kinds of reasons why I should forget the whole idea! I was too young. I was too small to stand the physical strain. I would need a protective apron and there were not the clothing coupons to spare for things like that. And – the coup de grace, so Mother thought – Eglinton Toll was far too dangerous a crossing in the blackout. Deflated, but far from defeated, I went to bed. Best to let Mother sleep on it, I decided. After all, Saturday was still three days away. Three days, for Mother's resistance to melt, I hoped.

Next day, at school, I established that Mary and Gina had encountered no parental objection and they were all set to start canteen work on Saturday. Jean already had received her parents' permission to do so. These facts were enough to scotch two of Mother's objections, for how could I be too young, when Jean was even younger and how could I be too small, when Mary was no bigger than I? Even so, there remained the problems of the apron and the negotiating of the crossing of Eglinton Toll in the dark. I shared my problems with Jean, Mary and Gina, expecting no more than sympathy really, for what practical help could they possibly give? In fact, Jean solved the problem of crossing Eglinton Toll in the blackout. Her own parents had been worried about that and Aunt Mary – bless her! – had come to the rescue with a promise to see Jean across the Toll to our homeward bus stop, although this gesture meant that she would have to re-cross to get the bus to her own home. When consulted about the idea of taking, not only her niece across the road, but her niece's three friends as well, the kind lady readily agreed. Another of Mothers objections was out of the way! There remained only the agony of the non-existent apron. I did not dare to go on canteen duty without protective clothing, for fear of getting my precious everyday clothes stained. Nor could I borrow an apron from Mother, for although she had enough of them to provide a clean apron for every day of the week, they were all out-size, whereas I was considered small for my age. I could only wait and hope for a sign that Mother had relented.

The sign was waiting for me when I got home from school on Friday. A brand new cotton apron, lilac, with flowers all over it and a big useful pocket trimmed with lilac bias binding, told me the good news. Mother smiled indulgently at my eagerness to try it on. The smile turned into a laugh when she saw the result! True, it fitted round the bust and the waist was passable, the side of the apron meeting, but not overlapping, at the back. But the length! It was almost to my ankles! Mother, having consented to part with precious coupons for the apron, had played safe and allowed for growth. She had bought a woman's size apron for me. A large tuck was clearly required if I was not to become the laughing stock of my friends. Never one to let me down, Mother spent her evening taking up my new apron by means of a generous tuck at the waist. Meanwhile, I dashed out of the house to tell Jean the good news.

Jean greeted the news with delight and gave me the details of how we were to get to the canteen the next day. It had been decided that we should travel together, all four of us – Jean, Gina, Mary and me – on the following afternoon, since for three of us, the canteen was new and strange. Jean was to act as our guide. We were to meet at the No. 5 bus stop at the top of the hill in Menock Road at 3.30pm. We had to bring our bus fare, our apron and a small note-book. This was for the purpose of recording, week by week, the hours that we actually worked at the canteen. We had to have the notebook signed each week by Mr Nelson in order to qualify for our National Service Badge when we had clocked up ninety-six hours. I am not sure what office Mr Nelson held. A genial, pleasant man with white hair, he seemed to be in overall charge of the Institute at Eglinton Toll and that included the Forces canteen.

Saturday dawned and I could scarcely eat my lunch for excitement, in spite of knowing that it might be eight o'clock that night before I sat down to my next meal. What I was embarking upon was a real adventure. In those wartime days we children were hardly ever farther from home than the church hall, a mile up the road, where the Guides met once a week. And we walked there and back, even on wet nights, for the evening buses were scarce. For me to be travelling as far as Eglinton Toll by bus, unaccompanied by an adult, was an event in itself, strange as it may seem to today's fourteen-year-olds. And as for meeting lots of strangers at a canteen, well, I could not have found courage to do it had my three friends not been with me. Even at fourteen, I was still painfully shy.

The planned rendezvous took place punctually and the four of us alighted from the bus at a stop near the canteen door. The Y.M.C.A. Institute building was at the corner of Maxwell Street and its swing doors were set diagonally on the corner. Once inside, we were confronted with a long, wide passage leading straight ahead to the canteen. To our right, was a stone staircase. Jean plunged confidently up first one flight then another, with the three rookies in her wake. We passed, on the first floor, a large hall with a stage and lots of chairs, then came residents' quarters, offices and on the top floor, the cloakroom where we were to leave our outdoor clothes and put on our aprons. Of Aunt Mary there was no sign.

There were several women in the room, getting ready for work and chattering while they did so. Silence fell when the four of us entered. I felt awful. Then Jean was recognised by a lady called Agnes and the ice was broken. Agnes introduced the other adults to us and Jean reciprocated on our behalf. I began to feel better. Our new colleagues proved to be typical Glasgow people, with the characteristic warmth and friendliness that made them ideally suited to working in a Forces canteen, where so many of the customers were literally strangers in a strange land. To these servicemen, even a warm smile or a word of greeting went a long way towards making them feel more at home. Agnes was a motherly soul and took us under her wing from the start. We need not wait for Aunt Mary to arrive, she said, for it was more likely that we should find her downstairs, already hard at work in the kitchen, although it was not yet four o'clock, the official starting time of the afternoon shift.

Agnes shepherded us downstairs and along the corridor that we had seen when we arrived. The passage was wide and quite long, terminating in swing doors. These opened on to a very large room, furnished basically but adequately with sturdy tables and stacking chairs. To the right of the doors, a counter stretched across the width of the room. Beyond the counter we could see – and smell – the kitchen. I guessed that chips were on the menu! How right I was. Before that shift was over I had learned that the canteen policy was "chips with everything", unless supplies of "everything" ran out, when it became "chips with nothing". The chips never ran out and no customer ever needed to leave the canteen hungry.

Agnes took us into the kitchen. The first person I saw was Jean's Aunt Mary, standing at one of the two sinks, peeling potatoes at a quite amazing speed. Beside her was a white enamel bucket, already full of peeled potatoes. The second fact I was to learn that afternoon was that Jean's Aunt Mary was known in the canteen as "The Potato Queen"!

The kitchen was not exactly spacious, but the staff made the most of it. Ranged along the wall opposite the canteen door, were a big urn heated by a gas ring, a conventional gas cooker with an oven, a working surface and the biggest chip fryer that I had ever seen. It made my mother's chip pan look like a toy. That completed the cooking department of the kitchen. On the walls at right angles to that one were, on one side, shelves and cupboards full of crockery, and on the other, a working surface that had a hand operated chip-cutter built in, two sinks and a draining board. The fourth wall, opposite the cookers, was taken up with a long table for laying dishes on when they had been dried. A big, wooden-topped table stood in the centre of the room. Apart from the door into the canteen, there was a door leading directly into the corridor, so that there was access to the kitchen without having to go through the canteen.

Aunt Mary introduced us to Maisie, the shift supervisor, who sat at the cash desk at the canteen door. I liked her. She was surprisingly young and she reminded me of pictures I had seen of Vera Lynn! Throughout the period from 1943 until 1945, when I lent a hand at the canteen, I never once heard Maisie raise her voice or get excited when things got hectic. She was the epitome of quiet efficiency. Maisie sized us up and, noting that Gina was the biggest of her four new helpers, delegated her to the chip-cutter! A good, strong right arm was needed, to keep thumping potatoes through the grid into the bucket below. By now, Aunt Mary was already filling her second bucket with peeled potatoes and the cook was shouting for chips. Gina fled, to start chipping for all she was worth!

Jean, Mary and I were directed to "do the bread". Jean had done this on her previous visit to the canteen so no explanation was needed from Maisie, who got on with detailing other jobs to staff members as they reported for duty. Some liked to serve at tables – for this canteen was not self-service – while others preferred to be backroom helpers in the kitchen. It all worked out very happily. There was not enough space in the kitchen for "doing the bread" and we used a long table, against a wall in the canteen itself, behind the counter, where we stood with our backs to the customers. This suited me nicely, as the very thought of facing a sea of strangers on the other side of the counter was enough to petrify me. Jean guided us through the kitchen, along the corridor and down a small, dark staircase, which led to the stores. There we found sacks and sacks of potatoes, tins of meat, packets of dried egg, cartons of margarine, crates of bottled sauce, any amount of tea, sugar, milk, jam and slab cake and what looked to me like a mountain of loaves or unwrapped plain bread. The quantity allocated to our shift had been set aside. I could not help thinking that our margarine alloca-tion looked far too small to cater for the stack of loaves that the three of us carried back to our station in the canteen. I had much to learn!

Jean uncovered what proved to be a slicing machine and showed Mary and me how to cut the bread into quite chunky slices. Mary turned the handle and I stacked the slices into three heaps, while Jean put some of the margarine in a deep enamel plate. She took this to the kitchen and put it under the urn, where the heat from the gas ring softened the margarine almost to melting point. She returned quickly to where we were waiting, each with a knife at the ready, all set to scrape the runny yellow margarine on – and off – the sliced bread. In future weeks the bread was to become our permanent job. It was a challenge to us, trying to spin out the margarine, but, no matter how frugally we spread the slices, each week there seemed to be more bread than margarine. Customers who came for a meal near the end of shift had to make do with dry bread. Sometimes, if they were lucky, there was some jam left.

The routine in the afternoon shift was to spend the time from four o'clock until about four forty-five preparing to cope with the avalanche of hungry customers that arrived after the finish of the football matches at Cathkin Park, Hampden and Ibrox. The crowds coming from and going to the cinemas and dance halls in the area also started flocking to the canteen about five o'clock and a queue would form in the corridor, when all seats were taken in the canteen.

The cook liked to have several batches of chips cooked and keeping hot in the oven as a reserve to be used at peak times, when demand for chips outstripped the rate at which fresh chips could be cooked. She also liked to have several basins – and I mean basins about the size of a washing-up bowl – full of reconstituted dried egg, all ready to be made into scrambled egg or omelettes. Dried egg, in one form or another, with cooked meat bearing the courtesy title "Spam", and the ubiquitous sausage, was all that the canteen offered as an accompaniment to chips. At the beginning of a shift and – with luck – throughout the entire three hours, a meal at the canteen consisted of a generous helping of chips with one of the available accompaniments, laced, if desired, with bottled sauce; a wad of bread and margarine, with jam, if required; a wedge of slab cake and a mug of tea. Towards the end of a shift on a busy Saturday, supplies of almost everything started to peter out because, although there was plenty in the stores, each shift had its own rigid allocation of supplies. The sole exceptions were chips and tea. These, apparently stemmed from a bottomless pit! But our shift seriously ran out of provisions only once, when I was there and the famine struck only a matter of minutes before the next shift was due to come on duty, bringing with them their allocation of fresh supplies.

When this was explained to the waiting queue of hungry men, they agreed to wait for the change of staff with great good humour. This docility of queues always amazed me during the war. They seemed to take the view that, after having waited for quite some time, another few minutes did not matter. From five o'clock onwards, the long corridor at the Y.M.C.A. Institute used to be packed with queuing servicemen, some of them cold and all of them hungry. Yet I never once witnessed any resentment at the delay.

That first afternoon, "operation bread and marge" was completed fairly smartly, considering our lack of experience. The slices were laid in great piles on platters at the counter, where the waitresses could get their own supplies when setting the tables. Maisie was not one to allow her staff to stand about in idleness. The last breadcrumb was no sooner swept up than Mary and I were dispatched to the kitchen to dry dishes. Jean was allotted a space at the big kitchen table and bidden to mix up a basin of the dreaded dried egg. This stuff came in different brands and experience taught us that some brands mixed smoothly and quickly, while others proved obstinate and lumpy. The taste appeared to vary too, for, on some days the dirty plates would come back from the canteen scraped bare, while on other days, we would be filling the waste bucket with rejected scraps of leathery textured egg. The only implement provided for mixing the dried egg was a simple wire whisk, so Jean, like Gina, needed a strong right arm and a lot of patience. As ever, Aunt Mary was at her sink, peeling happily. At the adjacent sink, another helper was elbow-deep in dirty dishes, which were beginning to pile up as the canteen got busier. Mary and I got stuck into the dish drying, replenishing wet towels from the enormous pulley that spanned the kitchen. The ceiling was high and the heat from the cooking was so great that tea towels, hanging there like bunting, dried rapidly. There was a gas geyser at the sink, so we had plenty of hot water to wash the dishes. I discovered that the dishwater on occasion could become quite revolting. It remained fairly clean provided that the debris on the dirty plates was scraped into a bucket before the plates went into the sink. But when things got really hectic, the staff whose duty was to clear the tables of dirty dishes had a habit of hastily plunging their piles of cups, saucers and plates, knives, forks and spoons, straight into the sink, much to my chagrin if I happened to be the dish-washer at the time. No sooner would these articles submerge than a disgusting film of flotsam would appear, consisting of leftovers of food, cigarette ends, spent matches and ash, while daubs of H.P. sauce and tomato ketchup coloured the water. This was changed for fresh hot water as frequently as time permitted, of course, but I began to see the point of jokes we often heard on the wireless about restaurants that served up the dishwater and called it Brown Windsor soup!

Maisie liked to vary the jobs to relieve monotony. Only Aunt Mary and the cooks kept to one task throughout the shift. That Saturday set the pattern for all our future spells of duty. When we were not doing the bread, chipping potatoes, mixing egg or washing or drying dishes, Gina, Jean, Mary and I would act as "runners", taking orders from the waitresses at the counter and passing them to the cooks. The plates were filled up on the big kitchen table and one of us would carry them on trays to the waiting waitresses. The runners were also responsible for keeping the four enormous brown enamel teapots filled up. These sat on a hot-plate on the counter, conveniently placed for the waitresses to pour out the tea as ordered. No wonder the troops called it "char". It sat there, stewing, getting stronger by the minute. Were I to be given a cup of such tea today, I should be unable to drink it, I am sure. Yet, after a few hours of hard work on the afternoon shift, I used to think that canteen char tasted like nectar. Jugs of milk and bowls of sugar sat beside the teapots and they, too, needed frequent replenishing.

One incident stands out in my mind, because it was so unusual. I would not have believed it, had I not seen it happen. A waitress called me to the counter and asked me to bring a pot of raspberry jam and a tablespoon. There was nothing unusual about that. Waitresses regularly replenished the jam dishes on the canteen tables. But, when I fetched the requested items, the waitress proceeded to spoon the jam liberally into two teacups. That done, she calmly topped up the cups with strong tea and stirred it all thoroughly. I knew I was staring but I could not stop myself. "What are you doing with that?" I asked her, not believing that the sticky mixture was drinkable. "It's for two of my regulars," the waitress replied, waving a hand in the direction of her corner table. There, smiling broadly, sat two American servicemen. "It's the only way they can swallow British tea," she explained. "They actually like it with jam." And off she went, to deliver the goods. There and then, I really did think I had seen everything! Life was certainly not dull at the Y.M.C.A. canteen.

We were very busy on our first day, but not so busy that we had to do without a tea break. Maisie made sure that first Jean and Gina and then Mary and I had ten minutes off, to sit down and have a cup of tea and a plate of chips. In future weeks we did not always manage to have a break, but, generally speaking, each member of the staff managed to find time for a cup of tea to revive flagging energy. It was all "go" and the three-hour shift flew past every week. We grew accustomed to the canteen routine as the Saturdays came and went and, gradually, we felt less tired at the end of a shift. But, on that first day, I confess we all had had enough when seven o'clock came round. The four of us, who had fairly flown up the stone staircase to the cloakroom when we arrived, climbed those same stairs at a markedly slower pace when the shift was over.

True to her word, once outside in the dark, Aunt Mary lined the four of us up at the pavement edge and led us across the wide black abyss of Eglinton Toll. In those days, the barrier that divides the Toll today had not been erected and five major roads converged, with dimly lit vehicles crossing diagonally, in a way that is quite impossible today. It was a truly scary place in the blackout and I could see why Mother had been worried. Once safely across, we waited at the No. 5 bus stop, which happened to be beside a monumental sculptor's yard. We leaned thankfully against the railings, glad to take some weight off our aching feet. Aunt Mary bade us goodnight, promised to see us the following week and vanished into the darkness, on her way to catch her own bus, at the other side of the Toll.

In future weeks, in fact, our newfound friend, Agnes, escorted us across the busy main roads, because she lived on that side of the Toll. She took this self-imposed duty most conscientiously, keeping it up until our very last day at the canteen, by which time I was nearly sixteen. When I protested that we were getting too old to be seen across the road, she paid no attention and marched us over as she had always done. She was a good soul, and one of the hardest workers on our shift.

In due course, Jean, Gina, Mary and I gained our Girl Guide National Service Badge, with date-strips for three consecutive years. We were not able to attend the canteen every week but we went whenever possible and put in far more hours than the required ninety-six per annum. Quite unexpectedly, we were each presented with another badge, when the Y.M.C.A. closed the Forces canteen. Each voluntary worker on the canteen staff received a metal badge, in the shape of a quatrefoil. Round the edge was a blue enamelled border, bearing the words "Voluntary War Service", picked out in gold. In the white centre of the badge the famous red triangle, bearing the letters "Y.M.C.A." was surmounted by a gold thistle. Those badges are probably of little, if any, monetary value today, but I treasure mine and the memories that it stirs.

17. BERRIES AND 'NEEPS

Although I was not allowed to sleep under canvas, there was one kind of camp that was not forbidden to me. That was the berry-picking camp, run by the school. Open to girls in Third Year classes and upwards, it had a parallel, the tattie howkin', which was for boys of similar age. I never knew why raspberries were reserved for girls, while potatoes were the prerogative of boys. Maybe berry-picking was considered to be too cissy for boys? Was tattie-lifting too tough for girls? Anyway, the two occupations and the two sexes were kept strictly apart.

As soon as I reached Third Year at school, in September, 1943, I began to look forward to the berry-picking camp at the end of the session. "You're wishing your life away, lassie!" Mother would remonstrate. But I was really keen to go to the berry-picking camp that summer. It spelt adventure, holiday, something different to do. And, for me, who had never been to a Guide camp, it promised the extra excitement that comes from being away from home on one's own, for the very first time. There were a few formalities to be gone through that session, however, before my dreams could be realised. The "Third Year Leaving Certificate" had to be obtained and that meant noses to the grindstone, from September until May. The constant pressure of work helped me to pass both the time and the examinations and, eventually, it was June, 1944.

Exciting things were happening and one in particular eclipsed even the July berry-picking camp for a while. Just as I can remember the events of 3rd September, 1939 with clarity, so 6th June, 1944 is impressed on my mind. I walked smartly home from school as usual, to snatch my lunch before repacking my bag for afternoon classes. The wireless was on, tuned to the inevitable *Workers' Playtime*. But, when it was time for the *One O'Clock News*, I stopped eating and began to listen. Something in the announcer's manner as he made the preliminary introduction made me hold my breath. I could sense that we were about to hear something sensational. Surely enough, the newsreader went on to announce that Allied Forces had landed, that very day, on the shores of Normandy. After nearly five years, the turning point in the war had been reached. Even I could feel it. In fact, Victory in Europe was to be declared eleven months later. We could not know that, of course, on 6th June, 1944. But, quite suddenly, there was the scent of certain victory and the promise of an end to the wearisome war. The nation's chin was up. Morale was high. Not even Hitler's secret weapons, the flying bomb and its successor, the rocket bomb, could wreck that.

I can remember walking back to school that afternoon, feeling the flutter of butterflies inside me, as though I were about to sit yet another important examination. The news had affected me in that way. I could not shake off the feeling that my life had taken a new direction. Perhaps, after almost five years of war, we could dare to think in terms of peacetime and allow our thoughts to wander over questions of how an ending of hostilities might affect our lives? It was strange to dwell on such thoughts that, only the day before, would have been dismissed as "wishful thinking". Peacetime life was a fascinating subject for me, for I could remember very little about what it had been like and, intuitively, I sensed that things would never be the same again. War would leave its mark on any new peace and I could only speculate on what the changes might be.

It must have been a warm, sunny day in Glasgow on 6th June, 1944 – D-Day, I distinctly remember that I was wearing my school blazer that afternoon. By nature a chilly mortal – my grandmother's good Scots word for me was "cauld-rife" – it took a fairly warm sun to persuade me out of my trench coat and into my royal blue blazer. Perhaps it was a good summer that year? I cannot remember. But I know that the berry-picking camp lasted for three weeks and I cannot recall ever wearing any waterproof clothing during that time.

If the whole nation felt high on the heady news of D-Day, it was brought back to earth with a salutary explosion a few days later, when the first of Hitler's flying bombs landed in the south of England. It was all we needed to make us realise that the war was not over yet. As far as plans for the berry-picking camp were concerned, they went ahead unchanged. We were assured that the flying bombs, launched in Europe, did not have a range long enough to reach the more northerly latitudes. We were deemed to be quite safe!

Towards the end of June, every girl who had volunteered to go berry-picking that summer was summoned to a meeting in the school. We had a chance to look at one another and find out exactly which girls were going to the camp and which were not. I think there must have been about thirty of us, some being old hands from previous camps and others, like Jean and me, being raw recruits. One of the mathematics teachers was to be in charge of the camp and, with typical precision and exactitude, she had drawn up a list of items that we were required to take. Nothing was overlooked. There was also a summary of travel details. We were to travel by train to Fife. The fruit farm where we were to work was on the outskirts of Cupar, but we were to be billeted in the disused Cults Manse, near Pitlessie village, some four miles from the town. Payment was to be made by the farmer at the rate of three halfpence a pound for every pound of raspberries that we picked. In turn, we were to pay the Education Department sixteen shillings a week, to cover our board and lodging. The teacher in charge would act as treasurer, keeping a tally of every girl's earnings over the three weeks and deducting the charge for board. The net earnings were to be paid to us at the end of the camp. It sounds like a pittance today, but in 1944 it felt like a fortune.

On the list of requirements there were several items that I did not possess. These were: a headscarf, a pair of dungarees and a sleeping bag. Because headscarves cost coupons, Mother cut up a summer dress that I had grown out of and she contrived to make, if not a head-square, a large triangle, neatly hemmed. This served the purpose quite adequately. I wore it in the fields all day for three weeks and when I brought it home after camp, the colours were quite faded with all the sunshine that we had enjoyed. Mother borrowed a very comfortable sleeping bag from our next door neighbour. It had been David's and he had used it for his climbing trips. There was no such thing as nylon filled with polyester then. The sleeping bag that kept me snug and warm at camp was of pale blue quilted cotton, filled with down. I cannot remember whether dungarees, being classed as working clothes, were free of coupons or not. Anyhow, Mother bought me a pair of pale blue denim dungarees, and Jean's mother bought her a pair of chocolate brown. I could not help noticing that both mothers chose dungarees to match their daughters' eyes!

The camp was scheduled to last for three weeks, commencing mid-July, to coincide with the raspberry harvest. My fifteenth birthday had occurred on 5th July and I felt that my sixteenth year was off to a good start. The days flew past and I was so excited that I remember almost nothing at all about our journey to Cults Manse. I know we all wore school uniform, navy gym tunic with royal blue sash, white blouse open at the neck (for we had no school tie then) and royal blue blazer. We each had one small suit-case. We went by train to Cupar station and I know we crossed the Forth Bridge. It was the first time I had ever done so and I found it an awesome experience to be so close to those enormous girders that look so deceptively delicate from a distance. Some of the girls in our party were running up and down the corridors of the train, throwing pennies out of the windows as we passed over the River Forth. What happened after we reached Cupar station I have not the faintest idea. My memory is blank. I suppose we took a bus – or maybe it was a lorry? – to the manse, but for all I remember, it might have been a magic carpet.

The manse itself stands out in my mind. To reach it, one left Cupar and took the Pitlessie road. After about four miles there was a country lane on the left, lined with hawthorn trees and flanked by fields of oats. This led to Cults church, then still in use, and Cults Manse, a large stone house, at that time not occupied. The wide entrance to the manse was flanked by stone pillars and the grounds were enclosed by a high stone wall. The gates opened to a courtyard. To the left was a substantial garage, with a concrete floor and doors pinned open. This airy building was empty, its only furnishings being a new-looking, slatted bench that ran, at table height, round the three walls. At the open entrance stood a pile of galvanised washing bowls, and a standpipe dripping cold water. Every home comfort! Who needed hot water anyway? This was camping life. At right angles to the garage/washroom was a long, low building with doors firmly closed. This proved to contain a number of Elsan cubicles. The indoor bathroom and toilet was for staff only!

Opposite the gates was the back door of the manse. Because it was so convenient, it was the only entrance in use. Beside the door was a lean-to extension that served to provide additional kitchen accommodation for us. Once inside the house, it proved to be roomy and rambling, like many another Scottish manse of that vintage. The ground floor contained a big kitchen and pantry, a corridor leading to a large lounge, a dining room with french windows, hall, front door and staircase. The front door led to a charming old walled garden with a sundial. The staircase led to the first floor bedrooms. Upstairs, the teacher's quarters were to the left and out of bounds to us. The pupils were to sleep in large dormitories and Jean and I found ourselves sharing a back room with six other girls of our own age. Our room-mates, like us, were all first-timers at the berry-picking camp. All that our room contained was eight camp beds. No curtains screened the two windows and no covering concealed the clean floorboards. No electric light switch was to be found. In fact, there was no electricity in the house! Yes, this really felt like camping.

I doubt if we ever missed the electricity. The summer days were long, we were all healthily tired after a day at work in the open air and we were in bed, fast asleep, before darkness fell on these July days. One of the school cleaners had accompanied our party, in the capacity of camp cook. She was a revelation. The meals and packed lunches that she turned out for her large and hungry "family" were a credit to her, particularly in view of rationing restrictions and the limitations of her kitchen. She did not seem to miss the electricity either.

Routine meals were breakfast, packed lunch taken in the field and dinner in the manse in the evening. A monitor system was worked out, giving us all a share in serving tables and washing up. We kept our own dormitories swept and tidy. But the very first job that we all had to do on arriving at the manse was to write a post-card to our parents, assuring them of our safe arrival. A stamped addressed postcard had been one of the items on our list of things to pack. It only remained for us to write a few words on it and hand it in to the camp supervisor for posting. She really had thought of everything!

The camp bed was surprisingly comfortable. My sleeping bag was in the luxury class. Yet I could not sleep a wink that first night. The certain knowledge that seven other girls around me were dead to the world did nothing to help. In my strange bed I wriggled and squirmed until morning, when the door was thrown open and a voice bade us get up. The news that a lorry was calling for us at eight thirty made us fairly jump out of bed. Putting on just enough clothes to make ourselves decent, we grabbed our towels and toilet bags and clattered down the uncarpeted stair, along the back corridor and out to the courtyard, where there was already a queue of girls at the standpipe. Jean and I helped ourselves to a washbowl each and joined the line. It did not take much time to fill the basins but it did take a certain skill. The force of the water was such that it tended to ricochet off the bottom of the basin and spray cold droplets over the waiting queue. With daily practice, we became adept at controlling the flow from the tap. After a day or two, we did not even raise a goose pimple at the thought of an early morning wash in cold water out of doors.

Exhilarated by the tingling water and morning air, we dashed upstairs to finish dressing, donning our new dungarees and long sleeved jumpers. On our feet, by order, were thick socks and rubber boots. Strange garb for mid-July perhaps, but it was well suited to the job we had to do.

The gong sounded and we all trooped to the dining room, where the trestle tables were laid for a two-course breakfast. First we sang Grace. "For health and strength and daily food, we give Thee thanks O Lord." Maybe I could not sleep, but I could certainly eat. I think we all did justice to that meal. We were just finishing when a shout went up – "The lorry's here!" It was precisely eight-thirty.

Tying on our headscarves, we filed through the back corridor. In the kitchen we could see an enormous pile of paper packages – our packed lunches. Cook had had a very busy morning. The lorry was parked in the lane at the gates and one by one we clambered in, using the rear mudguard as a foothold. Two of the staff travelled with us and so did the stack of lunches. We sang all the way to the fruit farm.

A puzzling item on our list of items to take to camp had been a stout leather belt. Its purpose became clear soon after we jumped from the lorry when it pulled up in a field of raspberry canes – rows and rows stretching as far as the eye could see. The foreman told each picker to help herself to two galvanised buckets, a large one and a small one. The smaller bucket was threaded on to the leather belt, which was then fastened round the picker's waist. Thus both hands were free to pick raspberries. We were paired off, each pair working up one row of canes, facing each other, keeping pace and picking steadily until the other end was reached. The berries were dropped into the small pail. This was decanted, when full, into the big pail, which was moved up the row with the picker. On reaching the end of the row, each pair walked along the field until they came to a row of canes that had no pickers. They worked their way back down that row. And so on, up and down, until twelve noon, when everything and everyone stopped for lunch. Before we could eat, we had to hand in our buckets and have our morning work weighed in the balance. As each girl's berries were decanted into the scale pan, our teacher made a careful note of the weight. Being new to the game, Jean and I had no idea of what weight of raspberries it should be possible to pick in a morning. But we did notice that the old hands among our colleagues were looking far from happy, and as we munched our sandwiches they told us why their faces were so long.

The raspberries were only just beginning to ripen. We had had to search for ripe fruit and this meant time wasted and low earn-ings. The experienced pickers reckoned that, at this rate, we would be hard pressed to earn our board and lodgings, never mind make a profit. I had thought I was doing quite well, picking seven pounds that morning, but apparently it should have been possible to pick three times as much. I had a lot to learn.

After dinner that evening, the camp supervisor asked us all to remain at the table because she had something to tell us. It had been agreed that raspberries needed another week to ripen. Accordingly, alternative arrangements had been made for our employment for the rest of that week. Turnip hoeing! We had been allocated to a farm in Newport-on-Tay, about twenty miles away, where we were to weed turnips and sugar beet. Payment would be made at the rate of ninepence an hour and no one over the age of eighteen years was allowed to go. In the absence of adult supervision, the senior girl in the camp was to be in charge. Because of the extra distance, the lorry was to come for us before eight o'clock each morning. So we had to get up earlier, too. This promised to be a real adventure. In spite of going to bed in a state of high excitement, I slept like a log.

The lorry ride next morning was like a journey into the unknown. The supervisor and her aides all gathered at the gates to see us off, clearly feeling anxiety that they were trying to hide. Once out of sight of the manse, we knew that we were on our own. Nan was in charge. She was seventeen but, with her small build, bright eyes and rosy cheeks, she looked younger than I did. The journey was much longer than the previous day's ride to the raspberry fields. After ten miles or so, the novelty began to pall. There are softer seats than the floor of a lorry and, when the legs cramp, there is nothing one can do but suffer the discomfort. But we kept singing, just the same. Fortunately, the lorry driver knew exactly where he was going. None of us did. We were quite lost. Then, in a flash, we got our bearings when the Tay Bridge – the railway bridge, of course – came into view and we could see MacGonagall's "Silvery Tay". We were in Newport.

The farm stood quite high, overlooking the Tay and, from our viewpoint, a train crossing the bridge looked like a toy. We were all familiar with the children's story "The Enormous Turnip". Now we were seeing an enormous field of turnips. It was like a sea of green and yellow, with the yellow predominating. We were soon to discover that it was our job to eradicate the yellow! Some job!

The lorry driver left us at the gate of the turnip field and a big, country-looking man, in bunnet, blue serge and boots, nicky-tams and all, came purposefully towards us, moustache bristling. In a strong Fife accent, he introduced himself as Jake, the foreman. He was to put us through our paces. He lined us up at the bottom of the field, facing up hill, our backs to the view of the Tay. We were allocated a drill of turnips apiece – Jake called them "neeps" – and we had to stand astride the shaws, waddling, penguin fashion, up the drill. Whereas penguins stand upright, we were literally bent double. Jake had informed us that the farm did not have hoes for us and we would just have to pull the weeds out by hand! So we got down to it and I mean got down to it. Thirty or so girls in rubber boots and dungarees, waddling in parabolic position, keeping in lines that would not have shamed the Guards at the Trooping of the Colour, must have been a sight for sore eyes. But all that we could see was a bird's eye view of a row of turnips as we progressed up the hill, head down, yanking out those yellow-flowered weeds that Jake called "skellochs".

Rapidly we discovered three drawbacks in our exciting new adventure. First, the skellochs had stings in their tails. Their stems were hairy and surprisingly prickly to the fingers that grasped them.

Years later, I learned that "skelloch" is a Scots word, meaning "yell"! Those weeds were well named. Second, the morning dew lay heavy on the turnip shaws and we had not taken many strides up our first drill before the bottoms of our trouser legs were sodden and clinging coldly to the bare flesh beneath. Most of the girls, like me, had rubber boots of only ankle length, so we could sympathise with one another in our muddy wetness. However, it must be said that this discomfort lasted only until the sun broke through to dry both dew and dungarees. The third drawback was backache. After working up a long drill, doubled up, it was an effort to straighten up again for the walk to the next, downhill row. By mid-morning, we looked like a huge advertisement for somebody's backache remedy, all holding our backs and grimacing horribly every time we stood erect.

Jake was quite relentless. He drove us up one drill and down the next, all morning. We soon realised that his bark was worse than his bite and that all we had to do to keep him happy was work hard. He had no time for slackers, especially when they were getting ninepence an hour.

During our few days of turnip weeding, we got to know the times of the trains crossing the Tay Bridge. None of us had a watch and the trains told us the time, marking out how long it was until lunchtime or until five o'clock, which Jake called "lousin' time", when the lorry would come for us.

On that first day at the turnips, the lorry was a welcome sight. We never felt the hardness of the floor. All we knew was that it was marvellous to sit down and rest our backs against the sides of the lorry. By the time we were within sight of home, we were all feeling fine again, if rather tired. Someone hit on the idea of playing a trick on the camp staff. Remembering their ill-concealed anxiety of that morning, we agreed to behave as if the work had been too much for us. When the lorry pulled up at the manse gate, instead of leaping out and getting washed and ready for dinner – for we were all ravenous – we sat still and kept very quiet. Just as we had foreseen, the staff came hurrying out to investigate our unnatural silence. We all leaned on one another, groaning softly, watching the teachers' expressions turn from mild concern to downright alarm! Then someone giggled and the game was up. We all had a good laugh. But we did not refuse when the teachers offered us a helping hand out of the lorry. We really were quite stiff. We would have appreciated a hot bath but this was camping life and a cold wash in the garage had to suffice.

The week passed very quickly. The yellow fields were restored to green and when we had finished the turnips we were pronounced experienced enough to be entrusted with the weeding of the sugar beet. It had to be treated with great care as any damage to the skin of the beet would cause it to "bleed". Jake got to know most of us by name in the course of those few days and when we waved from the lorry at twelve noon – lousin' time – on Saturday we felt we were taking leave of an old friend. We really liked Jake, in spite of his gruff manner.

On Saturday afternoon we were free to do as we pleased, within reason. Jean and I took a bus into Cupar and had a look round the town. We came back to Cults in time for dinner and I had scarcely begun to walk up the lane from the bus stop when I realised that I had left my purse on the seat of the bus. I had to borrow the price of a return ticket and go back into town that evening, this time to the lost property office at the bus station. Fortunately, I could remember to the last half-penny how much money the purse contained and, on describing my lost property accurately, I had it restored to me on payment of a salutary ten per cent of the contents. Honest folk, the Fifers.

On Sundays, during the camp, we all went to Cults church, next door, for morning service. I enjoyed those Sundays because they were so different from the working days. We were allowed to have a comparatively long lie in bed and a later than usual breakfast. Dungarees and jumpers were replaced by crisp and neat school uniform. The little church, in spite of its isolation, attracted a surprisingly large congregation and, on our first Sunday, there were many children present, for the Sunday school prize-giving. I soaked up the peace and quiet of those Sundays at Cults. Away from the workaday noises of the turnip fields or the fruit farm, we could listen to the larks singing, high above us, as we whiled away our precious leisure time in the manse garden, reading, or perhaps writing letters, or maybe just doing absolutely nothing, for the sheer novelty of it. Jean and I used to browse reverently round the old churchyard, reading the inscriptions on the gravestones. It was like reading a chapter of social history. Within a short walking distance of the manse, were some old and disused buildings, shaped like kilns. They stood on rising ground and, when we went to have a closer look at the buildings, we discovered that this gentle slope was thick with wild strawberries. My grandmother would have called them "averns". Some of us used to walk over there on a Sunday afternoon and pick the strawberries. It made a change from picking raspberries and we ate those sweet little berries from the hillside. We never ate the raspberries!

Various diversions were planned for our weekend time. One Saturday, we took part in a sports meeting, which had been arranged at the academy in Cupar, with teams from all the schools that were taking part in berry-picking in the area. One Sunday afternoon, our teacher sprang a surprise on us. A lorry drew up noisily at the manse gates during our lunch. We heard it and could not believe our ears. Surely we were not expected to work on a Sunday? It was the teachers' turn to laugh at our expense. I do not know how she managed it, but our supervisor had somehow arranged for our lorry to take us all on an afternoon outing to St Andrews. We spent the best part of that warm afternoon, sunbathing on the beach. I have been back to the old university town many times since that day, but only on that one occasion did I arrive on the back of a lorry!

It transpired that we were to use the lorry for yet one more purpose. Once a week, it called for us in the evening, to take us to the Baths in Cupar. Camping life or not, we were allowed to enjoy the luxury of a hot shower, once a week. When I returned home from camp, my father, who knew the town of Cupar quite well, asked me where the Baths were, declaring that he had not been aware that Cupar possessed such an amenity. In fact, the Baths were a temporary, wartime innovation. Their true function, I understand, was to decontaminate! They were spray baths and quite communal, in that they were not cubicle-ised. For this reason, quite a few of our campers declined to take advantage of the opportunity to have a weekly shower. Modesty forbade them, apparently. Personally, it troubled me not one whit to share a shower bath with a number of my fellow campers, considering any embarrassment, if such there was, a small price to pay for the sheer luxury of that wash in hot water. I know that a shower is not everyone's idea of a proper wash. A stalwart of the Fife Constabulary who was standing at the door as we entered the building, gave a snort when we asked him for directions to the spray baths. "Spray baths?" he said. "You'd be as well to try bathing in a saucer!"

After that first week of turnip weeding in the sunshine, the raspberries were ripe and ready in abundance. On the first morning back at the fruit farm, I picked twenty pounds. That was more like it. The berries went to a jam factory and our pickings were tossed into a huge container regardless of bruising or crushing. Condition did not seem to matter when the buyer was a jam manufacturer. It was a different story if the customer wanted "table" berries. One afternoon, an order came in for such a quality and I was chosen to pick these special raspberries. The foreman gave me an aluminium canister to hang at my waist, instead of the small galvanised bucket. I was instructed to select only the biggest and finest fruit. To compensate me for the time taken by such selectivity, I was to be paid at the enhanced rate of twopence a pound, for that special order!

The school camp was a most enjoyable diversion from the routine of wartime life in Glasgow, and I look back on those happy summer days with pleasure. Yet, even in the raspberry fields, we could not forget the war completely. The R.A.F. base at Leuchars was not far away and we grew quite accustomed to the sight of lorries, with badly damaged aeroplanes on their trailers, passing on the road that ran alongside the fruit farm. The chatter around us always seemed to die away momentarily as these lorries passed, carrying our thoughts back to the realities of wartime life – and death.

18. GOOD, BAD AND TERRIBLE

In June 1944, after the prize-giving and speeches, which marked the end of the school session, I had said goodbye to many of my friends who were leaving school. They seemed so numerous that I wondered how many of that Third Year would be coming back to form our new Fourth Year classes in September.

Meanwhile, there was the long summer holiday ahead. Thanks to the berry-picking camp, July passed in a flash. The sense of pending victory persisted. August raced along as each day seemed to bring news reports that fed the flames of my excitement. We heard that our troops had landed in the South of France. As if to underline the significance of this development, the BBC followed the announcement with the playing of the French national anthem. Paris was liberated. The French really were the free French again.

I followed the rapid progress of the Allied armies on Jean's *Daily Express* war map. This covered the best part of one wall in the living room of her house. I never visited Jean without looking at the map and reading the action story that the coloured flags and pins had to tell. I never failed to feel a sense of awe at the visual evidence of how widely the war and its trail of destruction had spread since that Sunday in September 1939.

Jean, Marian and I had much in common, and so had our parents, because of their similar circumstances. But, in one respect, my parents were quite different. Jean's family lived with war maps on their walls. Marian's parents had portraits of the King and Queen and the Prime Minister looking down at them as they sat in their living room. In our house, there was to be found no such evidence of the troubled times in which we were living. When my father finally arrived home by bus each night from his work, which was closely tied up with war and its weapons, he liked to close the door on the blackout and, in a sense, shut out the war. He could relax in the peace of his home. Intrusive war maps and patriotic portraits were not for him. Certainly, he took a close interest in the progress of the war, through newspapers and wireless. But these could be put aside or switched off at will and that was how Father liked it.

We did not dream of switching off the on-the-spot reports from BBC war correspondents. Such drama-packed news bulletins seemed to barge into our home and grip us by the throat. These men took death-defying risks to bring their listeners a true picture of fighting as it took place. I remember one reporter – I think it was the late Stewart MacPherson – broadcasting from a plane while enemy guns were firing all around. He broke off momentarily, with a gasp, as he was hit. But he carried on with his recording, nevertheless. My sister greatly admired the late Guy Byam, another BBC war correspondent, and she noticed that we had not had any reports from him for some time. Later, we learned that he had been killed, as were many Allied troops, at Arnhem.

That setback at Arnhem roughly coincided with our return to school, in September. Our Forces were finding tougher resistance and their struggle seemed to symbolise for me the long hard slog that lay ahead of us at school as we set out upon the Senior School course, which would culminate in the all important "Highers" in 1946.

We found, on reporting at the beginning of the autumn term, that about a hundred pupils had returned for Fourth Year. All of us hoped to earn a pass in the Senior Leaving Certificate examinations and we had all been interviewed earlier and had our individual courses mapped out. In those days, one had to take a recognised "group" of subjects and, although reasonable choice was available, English and arithmetic were compulsory for all candidates. If one failed in English, the certificate was not awarded, no matter what other passes were obtained. Because Kings Park was a new senior secondary school, it had a reputation to build. What kind of reputation that would be was up to us. We had a strong sense of loyalty and this drove us to work especially hard. The target was a one hundred per cent pass, nothing less.

The Fourth Year had been split into three classes – "Girls", "Boys" and "Technical". These were known, officially, as "4G" "4B" and "4T". Quite naturally, the girls renamed the classes "Good", "Bad" and "Terrible"!

I found the specialised Fourth Year work a refreshing change from the all-embracing curriculum of the first three years. To my intense relief, the subjects that I had studied previously from compulsion and not from choice could be dropped from my senior course. The discipline of Latin had been a sore trial to me. As for science, I found the very smell of the laboratories barely tolerable. I can truthfully say that I hated every minute that I spent in science class. With great glee and never a backward glance, I abandoned Latin and science in favour of art and the history of architecture.

This decision met deep disapproval. The headmaster warned me that I was wasting my life, throwing it away on something so ephemeral as art, a subject that he considered frivolous. He had Honours Degrees in mathematics and science himself. His logical mind could not fathom how I, when faced with picking one subject from Latin, science and art, should choose the latter when my examination marks had always been higher in both Latin and science than in art! At that time, art was all too often regarded as a subject to be taken only by pupils who were academically unsuited to anything "better". I did not fit that description. Hence the headmaster's consternation. Backed solidly by my parents, I stuck to my guns and to my original choice. As events were to prove, it was just as well that I did.

Probably because I was genuinely enjoying my school work – perhaps for the first time in my life – I sailed through the Christmas examinations and took first place in my year. I felt all set to do the same in the summer term, but Fate took a hand.

Halfway through the Easter term, I contracted chickenpox. At the age of nearly sixteen years, I took it very badly indeed. Our family doctor, a man of many years' experience, declared mine to be one of the worst cases that he had ever seen. I bear some of the scars to this day. Contact with the outside world was forbidden. My schooling was in a state of suspended animation for the duration of my illness, and that was six long, uncomfortable weeks.

I was pronounced fit to return to school just as school was breaking up for the Easter holidays. Jean and Marian rallied round to help bring my work up to date. There were reams of history notes to write up, page after page of French vocabulary to learn, a fair portion of history of architecture to catch up on and some mathematics that, in the textbooks, looked like unintelligible hieroglyphics. For two whole weeks, while my school-mates were on holiday, I worked at home. By the time school resumed after Easter, I had almost caught up with my classes. Thank goodness I chose art, I thought. Had I taken Latin or science, I could never have caught up and could have had to repeat my Fourth Year, surrounded by a bunch of "kids" a whole year my junior. I would have gone to any lengths to avoid such ignominy!

I had been back at school barely a fortnight when, one evening, Mother told me to put my coat on, because we were going to see the doctor. This came as a considerable surprise to me. I had noticed that Mother had been giving me a lot of hard looks ever since I had come home from school that afternoon, but I had not guessed what was in her mind. Going to the doctor did not make sense. Apart from a slight headache, I did not feel ill. Why throw away money? (A visit to the doctor's consulting room cost 4/6 in those pre-Health-Service days, while a house call by the doctor was charged at the rate of 7/6 a visit. Medicine was extra, too. My long drawn out chickenpox had already cost my parents a tidy sum.) Mother was adamant. I looked flushed, she said, and she thought I might be coming out in a rash. I did feel warm, I had to agree, protesting nevertheless that that was only natural on a lovely April evening. My protests were to no avail. They got me nowhere with my mother. Or, rather, they got me to the doctor's consulting room.

I was very attached to our old family doctor. Avuncular, almost Pickwickian with half-moon glasses and a watch and chain, he was a man who inspired confidence, dispensed comfort and sound advice, who listened patiently to the most trivial worry and who always made me feel better for having spoken with him. He had a loud, ringing voice, a hearty laugh and a direct approach. He could express blunt opinions straight from the shoulder, yet he had an ideal bedside manner. He had all the time in the world for patients who were genuinely in need of his services but he could not suffer people who merely wasted his precious time. With misplaced confidence, I felt sure that Mother was about to receive a reprimand for making a fuss about nothing. I ought to have known better.

Dumbfounded, I heard the doctor say "You've got German measles." I did not want to believe my ears. I could not afford another spell off school. But the laws governing infectious diseases could not be disobeyed. I had to be excluded from school for at least two weeks. And I did not even feel really ill, only angry and bitterly disappointed. The cards seemed to be stacked against me. My chance of being Dux of Fourth Year had finally eluded me. I should be lucky even to pass the summer examinations, never mind to take first place.

Perhaps I really was more ill than I thought I was. During my long spell in bed with chickenpox I had grown a lot. After having been the third smallest girl in my year, I was now about average height. Mother said I was outgrowing my strength to say nothing of my clothes. I certainly seemed to have very little energy and the slightest exertion tired me – quite a change for me, for I had always been in the school gymnastics display team. It transpired that I was so debilitated that I was off school for not two weeks, but three.

Officially, I was not allowed any visitors, because of my infection. Fortunately for me, my form teacher, who had supervised the berry-picking camp, ignored protocol. She decided, and rightly so, that a little occupational therapy would do me no harm. As our house was only a few minutes' walk from the school, she voluntarily gave up her free periods, several times a week while I was off, and came to visit me armed with textbooks, pencils and paper. After half an hour's intensive tuition in algebra, geometry and trigonometry, she would depart, leaving me with enough homework to keep my busy until her next visit. She was a gifted teacher and I owe her a great deal.

While I was hovering on and off the sick list, the world outside was witnessing continuing drama. President Roosevelt had died suddenly, news that sent shock waves rippling round the world. How would the comparatively unknown vice president, Mr Truman, cope in the wake of his famous predecessor? we wondered. Before that remarkable month of April, 1945 was over, two other national leaders had left the face of the earth. Mussolini was shot in Italy and, soon afterwards, Adolf Hitler took his own life in Germany. It could only be a matter of days until the war in Europe was over, we felt sure.

In fact, the end of the war in Europe was declared officially on 8th May, 1945. We called it, not V-Day, but VE Day. It reminded us that, in this World War, there was still heavy fighting taking place outside Europe. Our troops were at peace on the continent, but lives were still being lost in the Far East. Japan was as yet undefeated. Perhaps it was the thought of the conflict continuing in unspeakable jungle conditions, perhaps it was my run-down state of health, but the Victory celebrations, which I had so looked forward to, failed to arouse in me the anticipated sense of elation.

Back at school, the only gesture of celebration that I can remember concerned the window net that had clouded our vision throughout the war. While our teachers turned a blind eye, our entire class fell upon the loathsome net, picking at it with our nails, our rulers, our pens, in fact with anything at all that would prise the offensive material from the glass. The staff were as pleased as the pupils to be able to see through the school windows properly, for the very first time. It was almost as great a pleasure as the ending of the blackout.

As far as Kings Park School was concerned, Victory-in-Europe Day in May was followed by Victory-at-Hampden Day, in June. One of the school football teams met a team from St. Mungo's Academy in the final of an inter-schools competition. St. Mungo's played well. Their supporters shouted and blew trumpets. They even let off a squib or two. But all in vain. Kings Park won the match and the shield. It was St. Mungo's misfortune that our goal-keeper that day was Ronnie Simpson, who was later to play for Scotland.

The end of term examinations were duly held. Of course, I did not take first place as I had hoped to do, in the distant days of December. Yet neither did I fail, as I had feared I might, after my recent illnesses. I took nineteenth place in my year. Normally, for me, that would have been a disgraceful performance, but, in the circumstances, I was well pleased and so must the staff have been, for none of my teachers uttered a single word of reproach.

19. JUBILATION AND TRIBULATION

Having grown accustomed to the pattern of wartime life, I could not help feeling that I was being pushed into peacetime ways all too abruptly. I needed time to get used to it. I had scarcely come to terms with the events of 8th May, 1945 when people were beginning to talk of a general election. Because of the war, the parliament that had been in session in 1939 had continued without dissolution. People of my age had come to regard it as a permanent institution. We had quite forgotten that the British Parliament was supposed to have a limited life. I could not remember the previous election at all.

The general election that duly took place on 5th July, 1945 stands out in my memory because it was held on my sixteenth birthday. Of course I was still five years too young to have a vote, but I was sufficiently interested in current affairs to pay attention to the election campaign. The game of party politics was strange and new to me. Unlike modern polls, when the final result is known within twenty-four hours or so, in 1945 we had to wait for about three weeks to know the outcome of the election. This was because British service personnel serving overseas were entitled to vote and assembling their completed ballot papers took some time. It must have been about the end of July, 1945 when we learned that the Labour Party had won the election convincingly. Mr Churchill, the leader in war, had been rejected in his bid to be the pioneer of peace. Mr Attlee was the new Prime Minister.

So wrapped up were we all in these new and important developments on the Home Front that the war in the Far East seemed to slip into obscurity for a time. Only the worried relatives of those whose misfortune it was to be involved in the fighting out there remembered the "forgotten army". Once the election was over, our attention turned again to the war map of the Far Eastern zone. In a matter of only a few days and with dramatic suddenness came the news that the Americans had dropped an "atomic bomb" on the densely populated Japanese city of Hiroshima, causing destruction on a scale that was beyond my imagination. I remember the date. It was 6th August, my father's birthday. The very name "atomic bomb" was new to me. I could remember reading an article in *The Children's Newspaper* years earlier, about man's attempt to split the atom. Not being of a scientific turn of mind, I had not been able to grasp why he wanted to do so; I had not heard that eventually he had been successful; and certainly I had never realised what the consequences of splitting the atom might be. Now that I knew, I was appalled. My creeping goose pimples of horror had not subsided when there was news of a further atomic explosion, this time in Nagasaki. Japan had had enough. Some people said she had had more than enough. Her choice seemed to be annihilation or capitulation. She surrendered and the war ended officially on 14th August, 1945. We called it VJ Day.

Swept along by the landslide of major events that had taken place within a few weeks of my sixteenth birthday, I and all the rest of my family had overlooked something. I had omitted to register at the Ministry of Labour and National Service!

There were two types of civilian identity card, junior and senior, and the junior was exchangeable for a senior card at the age of sixteen. Under the Registration of Boys and Girls Order, 1941, I was supposed to have presented myself, on my sixteenth birthday, at our local National Registration Office for the purpose of "registering" and exchanging my old identity card for an adult blue one. According to form ED431C that was issued to me subsequently, the government required sixteen-year-olds to register "so that they might be helped to find the best way of fitting themselves to do their duty as citizens and of assisting the national effort". I had forgotten to do so. What would happen to me? There was only one thing to be done – go to the National Registration Office without further delay and face the music. I was at fault and I could not deny it.

To my relief, the Office turned out to be in familiar territory. It was in Turriff Street, quite near the Y.M.C.A. canteen, and I knew exactly how to get there. Off I went, hoping for the best while fearing the worst. Having had no previous experience of dealing with a government office, I did not know what to expect. I imagined it might look something like a bank, with a long counter and polite people ready to be of help. Wishful thinking! Certainly, the room that I entered was about the size of our local bank, with a long shiny wooden counter, just like the one in our bank. There, the resemblance ended. Behind that counter was no polite bank clerk. The virago who was glaring at me as though I had no right to be there proved to be a very uncivil civil servant. In vain, I tried to control the quaver that betrayed my nervousness as I explained to her why I was late in registering. I tried to proffer a lame apology, but such sweetness was wasted on that desert air. Nothing I could say could counteract the asperity of that woman's tongue. I did not enjoy her lecture. Finally, she barked several questions at me concerning the youth organisations that I attended. Inevitably, she filled in a form, her manner all the while suggesting that I was responsible for giving her the labours of Hercules. Picking up the blue card, which she sent scudding across the counter, I fled. I have that identity card to this day. It bears the date-stamp 11th August, 1945, and is kept in one of the wallets that were sold for the purpose. It was carried with me wherever I went, until 1952 when identity cards were abolished in Britain.

School resumed in September. Fifth Year was upon us, with the dreaded Highers due in the spring. An unpleasant shock awaited us. Because it was now peacetime, the temporary arrangements that had been in force during the war concerning the Highers had been withdrawn. The old peacetime regulations and stringent standards were to be applied when our turn came to sit the examinations in 1946. The fact that we had received wartime education did not seem to have been taken into account. No quarter was to be given.

During the war, Scotland had been divided into areas and a local examination had been set for each area. The candidates were supervised during the examinations by their own teachers. As far as I can remember, there were no oral examinations. Once the written paper was done, the strain was lifted. All that remained for the candidate to do was wait for the area headquarters to issue the results.

Under peacetime conditions there was one set of examination papers for the whole of Scotland. Independent invigilators were sent out to supervise the examinations, while the teaching staff, excluded from the room, could only wait outside, as tense with anxiety as the candidates themselves. The written papers were sent to Edinburgh for correction and the ordeal did not end there. There were oral examinations to follow. These were spread over a period of weeks because there were a lot of subjects for H.M. inspectors to cover and many schools to be visited throughout Scotland. The agony was prolonged! These oral examinations were of great importance, especially to candidates who were "on the border-line" in the written paper. Such unfortunate beings could pass or fail on the strength of the performance they put up at the oral examination. Clearly, we were destined for a nerve-wracking Fifth Year.

I was sixteen years old when that school year began. Sitting alongside me were several boys who had reached the all-important age of eighteen years. In 1945, boys were eligible to be called up for National Service at that age, but a signed statement from the headmaster certifying that a boy was studying for the senior leaving certificate examinations was enough to gain deferment of call-up. This arrangement inadvertently gave the headmaster the means of persuading any lazy eighteen-year-old youth to work! It was a case of "concentrate on your lessons or else…!", the alternative being the implied, though unspoken, threat to cancel deferment. It worked like a charm. The "idle Jacks" got their heads down and kept them down – except for one isolated instance when temptation proved too much.

News had broken that a rare treat was in store for the football fans in Glasgow. Rangers F.C. were to play the famous Moscow Dynamo team at Ibrox. Sensational news! Every boy in Fifth Year wanted to see that match. It was taken for granted that it would be a Saturday game and, when the exact date of the fixture was published, consternation reigned. It was to be a mid-week match, played just before our preliminary examinations – a dress rehearsal for the Highers – were due to take place. A keen football fan himself, the headmaster sensed what was likely to happen and decided to nip the potential truancy in the bud. He did not send a message to the form teachers as he often did in the case of minor everyday matters. Instead, he assembled the entire Fifth Year in one room and addressed us personally. His words were very much to the point. The gist of his message was "attend that match at your peril!" Pointing out that a double period of mathematics followed by French dictée practice would prove to be of more lasting benefit to us than any fleeting enjoyment we might hope to glean from a football match – even THAT match – he promised to bring dire retribution upon the head of anyone foolish enough to disobey him. We knew that he meant what he said. He always meant what he said. We could all forget the football.

The day of the match dawned. I doubt if anyone in the City of Glasgow saw the actual break of day. It was foggy. Very foggy. We all went to school to get on with our Higher mathematics. All, that is, except John. His desk, in the middle of the room, was conspicuously empty, and try as we might, the rest of us found it hard to keep our thoughts on the subjects in hand. John was eighteen. Had he thrown away both his deferment and his chance to gain the Senior Leaving Certificate for the sake of a football match? Foolish boy! The headmaster came in to check that his wishes had been obeyed. His face was like thunder when he went out. John's fate was sealed, we were sure.

In fact, John was saved by the Glasgow fog. Normally a cocky lad, he was a sadly chastened one when he came to school next day. From shouting in the fog, he had a very sore throat, which left him with no speaking voice whatsoever, and, for good measure, he was suffering the discomforts of a severe head cold. Moreover, although he had paid for his ticket and had stood on the terracing at Ibrox Park for the duration of the match, he had seen no more of the game than we had, sitting at our desks in Kings Park. I am ashamed to admit that we all had a good laugh at his expense. He had kicked against the pricks and had come off worst of all. To add to his misery, he was on the carpet in the headmaster's room to answer for his sins. The headmaster was known behind his back as "Hitler". Fortunately for John, the nickname stemmed more from the sleek dark hair and small black moustache than from the headmaster's attitude to those who had crossed him. Deep inside our "Hitler" beat the heart of a football fan. The miscreant's deferment was not cancelled. I think the headmaster felt that John had been the architect of his own punishment.

The preliminary examinations were tough, so tough that passing them was a satisfying experience. It left us with a feeling of solid achievement. Because we had all worked so hard for the sake of the school's reputation, everyone had done quite well in this last big hurdle before the real thing in March. As the exact marks gained in the Highers were never made public, the marks awarded in the "Prelims" determined the prizewinners for that year. I realised that two prizes would be coming my way at the end of June. All things considered, it was a satisfactory approach to the ordeal ahead.

The Highers timetable was published, covering a period of fifteen days. The starting date, 13th March, did not bode well for the superstitious. By pure chance, all the subjects that I was to sit were timed to take place within the first ten days and I found myself "on holiday" for several days at the end of the timetable while examinations in subjects that did not concern me took place. I was glad of the breather, for I had developed a heavy cold and was feeling below par.

The Highers were behind me and I did my best not to brood about my performance. It was quite pointless to keep going over and over the questions as if they were so many worry beads. The die was cast and nothing could be changed. To be honest, I had a disappointing sense of anticlimax. The "Prelims" had been so very hard that the actual Highers had seemed tame by comparison. I found myself asking, "Is that what all the fuss was about?" Others felt as I did. Somehow – I cannot explain why – we felt cheated!

Over the ensuing weeks, with painful slowness, the Orals dragged on. The English Oral concentrated almost entirely on one girl. On her past record, her success had never been in doubt. Yet, on the day when it mattered most, she must have done herself less than justice. Poor thing, she suffered a very thorough grilling from the visiting inspector. Those of us who were not in the glare of his attention could only sit in our places and will her to pass. (In time, we learned that she did.) I, who had not been asked a single question, came out of that room feeling as limp as a wet rag.

The mathematics Oral was a misnomer. It proved to be another written paper. To me, the equations looked like Chinese and I was supposed to be good at mathematics! I was convinced that I had failed miserably. (I passed.)

The French Oral came, but passed me by. A 'flu bug pole-axed me, a few days before the inspector's visit, and I was sent home early from school because I was so unwell. I was sweating it out at home, in bed, when I should have been doing the same thing in the examination room. Our doctor had to provide a medical certificate (price 1/6!) to prove that my absence was due to genuine illness.

At last, the Senior Leaving Certificate examinations for 1946 were over. The ordeal of waiting had still to be endured.

20. CELEBRATIONS

We had celebrated VE Day in May, 1945, before there had been time to remove the blackout hoods from all the city streetlights. We had celebrated VJ Day in August, 1945, although many of our servicemen had been unable to join in the fun because they were still overseas. It was decided in high places that a special day should be set aside for the purpose of a national celebration of victory, at a time when the British people had got their breath back after the long struggle. The day selected was 8th June, 1946, and it was called, simply, V-Day.

It was marked in the cities, towns and villages by appropriate peace time festivities, such as floodlighting, fireworks, bonfires, parades and dancing in the streets. In Glasgow, there was a grand scale Victory parade, which started in Blytheswood Square and ended in George Square, where the Lord Provost took the salute. Making up the marching column were contingents from all the Services, including representatives of nurses, firemen, land girls and indeed of all who had helped to win the war. The youth organisations were also represented. That was where I came in. The Girl Guide Association contingent was composed of two girls from every company in the city. My canteen colleague, Gina, and I were detailed to represent our own Sea Ranger crew, which we had helped to form when we became too old for Guides.

For several evenings before V-Day, Gina and I joined the other Guide representatives in a city drill hall, to be put through our paces by a Guider who had recently returned from the Women's Services. She really licked us into shape. So soon after my bout of influenza, I was quite exhausted after an evening's square-bashing on that enormous concrete floor. But we had to be well drilled and smartly turned out because we were appearing in the parade alongside true professionals from the Navy, the Army and the Air Force.

For a reason that now escapes me, every girl in the Guide contingent was instructed to take a coat with her on the day of the parade. Perhaps it was to protect our uniforms from soiling en route from home to the assembly point, which, in our case, was the Boy's High School in Elmbank Street? I have no idea. But coats we had to have and a perfect nuisance they proved to be. When we all assembled in the high school – Sea Rangers, Land Rangers, Air Rangers and Guides – we were told to leave our coats in one of the classrooms, for collection after the parade. Thereafter, we marched to Pitt Street, which was our official marshalling point.

The youth organisations took up position at the end of the parade and we could not see the head of the long column. It was a long way ahead of us, in Blytheswood Square. We stood in our places, waiting for the official starting time and feeling inside us the faint, excited, fluttering of butterflies. Someone said it was like waiting in the wings for the curtain to go up on a theatrical performance, for we could hear the bands playing and the buzz from the crowds of spectators, although they were not yet in view.

The parade moved off and we swung into our stride. On either side of the column, the city pavements were packed with smiling, happy, people. The atmosphere was quite exhilarating. When we reached George Square, it looked like a swaying sea of faces, flags and flowers. The Lord Provost, with the city councillors, added a further splash of colour in their ceremonial robes of scarlet and ermine. For the first time, I saw the City Fathers in all their formal finery and, from my place in the parade, I enjoyed a close-up view. Carried along as we were on the beat of the happy music that accompanied the parade, the distance from Blytheswood Square to George Square had seemed deceptively short. All too soon, the music stopped and we were standing, at attention, in the contrasting quietness of John Street, behind the City Chambers, screened from the dispersing crowd. Only when I obeyed the command, "Parade! Dismiss!" did I begin to feel tired. There was a bus stop for home nearby. I had turned towards it when Gina, ever practical, stopped me. I had forgotten about my coat, far away in Elmbank Street. Just to think of the walk back made me wilt. Our contingent walked in little groups back to the Boy's High School, purposefully pushing our way through crowds of people who did not seem to be going anywhere. Our route was mainly uphill and, when we reached the classroom at last, I knew that I was tired. I also knew that, there in the West End, I was a long way from my Southside home. The city traffic had been disrupted by the parade and it was quite some time before we managed to get a bus that was going in our direction.

When I did reach home, Mother offered to make me a very welcome cup of tea. While she was doing that, I went upstairs to change out of my uniform. I sat down on the edge of my bed. It felt good. I leaned back on the springy mattress – and I fell fast asleep! Just like that! I must have gone out like a light. The tea made, Mother came looking for me. Finding me asleep, she draped a quilt over me and left the room. Sleep was better for me than tea at that point, she decided wisely. Two hours passed before I surfaced!

National holidays were not meant to be spent sleeping, however, and I gave myself a shake and stood up. After a good wash and a reviving meal, I felt ready for anything. Our whole family had caught the spirit of the Victory celebrations and we agreed that we should all go out together that evening, to see what was going on in the town. We took a bus into George Square and joined the throng of Glasgow citizens in celebration. Darkness did not fall until quite late that evening, but willingly, we waited, for the sake of the almost forgotten sight of floodlit buildings and lights, lights and still more lights. People were dancing and singing in the streets, linking arms with total strangers. If they did not know how to dance, they played children's games, like "Ring-a-Roses" and "Bee Baw Babbity". I cannot recall that we did anything in particular. It was just a marvellous feeling to be part of a happy crowd on a summer evening, breathing the air of freedom, which victory had preserved for us. It was long after midnight when, ignoring the night bus service, our family voted to walk home.

Arm in arm, we made our way among the many other people who were still in the streets at that late hour. We took the shortest route home and even that was several miles. It led us through streets that I should have avoided, had I been alone. But Father was with us, as straight and tall as any Guardsman, and we walked in safety by his side, in the light from the streetlamps of peacetime Glasgow.

The nation had fought its battles and had won through to victory. I had fought my own personal battle, for my Senior Leaving Certificate. Had I won? I was still waiting to hear the result.

When we went back to school after V-Day, every pupil was given a card bearing a crested copy of a message from His Majesty King George VI. It was dated 8th June, 1946 and read as follows:

To-day, as we celebrate victory, I send this personal message to you and all other boys and girls at school. For you have shared in the hardships and dangers of a total war and you have shared no less in the triumph of the Allied Nations.

I know you will always feel proud to belong to a country which was capable of such supreme effort; proud, too, of parents and elder brothers and sisters who by their courage, endurance and enterprise brought victory. May these qualities be yours as you grow up and join in the common effort to establish among the nations of the world unity and peace.

George R.I.

On the back of the card was a list of important war dates, beginning with the German invasion of Poland on 1st September, 1939 and ending with the British forces re-entering Singapore on 5th September, 1945 – stepping stones through six years of the nation's history.

We had received a message from His Majesty. We, in the Fifth Year, were still waiting for a message from Edinburgh. Day after day we would brace ourselves – and no news would come. Then, one morning near the end of June, the entire Fifth Year was assembled.

The headmaster and all the heads of departments were waiting for us, with solemn faces that yielded no clue to our anxiously searching eyes. In silence broken only by the thudding of a hundred hearts, the full name of each candidate was read out, in alphabetical order, the name being followed by one terse and fateful word, either "Pass" or "Fail". After every announcement, a sigh could be plainly heard. Mostly, it was of relief, for the school had done very well in its first attempt at the full dress Senior Leaving Certificate examinations. Sadly, there were tears of disappointment mingling with our tears of joy, for one or two did not make the grade.

Nowadays, I believe that the results of the "Highers" are sent privately to pupils, by post. In my case, the outcome was announced for all the class to hear. Not only did they all hear of our success or failure, they also heard our full names. Some of these made eyebrows rise. Secrets kept closely guarded for years were revealed. We learned that a girl whom we had known for eleven years as "Audrey" was actually called "Jean". Another, whom we had called "Joyce" had been baptised with the name "Francesca". Quite a few boys also had Christian names that had never been aired in school until that day and, in certain cases, that was not surprising! When, years later, I had to help my husband choose names for our daughters I remembered the discomfiture of some of those boys and girls who had been saddled by their parents with Christian names or initials that proved to be a source of acute embarrassment to them, and I tried to avoid the obvious pitfalls. With a surname like mine, one cannot be too careful!

All that remained to look forward to in that final session at school was the closing ceremony, with speeches and prize-giving. This was always held in Kings Park Parish Church. The First Year pupils sat near the front, the Second Year in the rows behind them and so on, with the Fifth Year occupying the back rows. That meant that the senior prizewinners had a very long walk to the dais. Mercifully, I was spared that ordeal – which was enough to turn the knees to jelly – because I was in the choir. This enabled me to sit in the second front row. When my name was called I merely slipped from my place, took only a few steps, bobbed a curtsey, shook hands and I was back in my place again. What a relief!

I had further cause to be glad. The previous year, I had won a prize for French. This year, I had not and I had felt disappointed at being ousted by a rival – until the actual ceremony changed my outlook. The speeches over, the headmaster invited the guest speaker's wife to present the prizes. This lady proved to be a native French speaker. Her face lit up with pleasure each time a prize for French was announced, and she engaged each recipient in torrential French conversation. I had faced enough ordeals for one year. Conducting a French conversation in the hearing of the whole school would have been the last straw. My rival was more than welcome to her trophy!

End of term was an emotional occasion for those of us who were severing our ties with the school that had been part of our lives for twelve years. The day before the prize-giving, we had gone round the staffroom taking our leave of individual teachers, but that was nothing compared to the thought of saying goodbye to our fellow pupils. Having been through thick and thin together, parting was not easy. Long after the rest of the school had dispersed to begin another long summer holiday, our Fifth Year was to be found standing in ever-changing groups outside the church, as we mingled, bidding final farewells in the June sunshine. Some of these old school friends still keep in touch with me. The majority, I have never seen again.

21. FROM THE GREENHOUSE TO A VERY COLD FRAME

In some respects, secondary school resembles a giant greenhouse. It provides the atmosphere and conditions that enable the young and tender to be brought to maturity. But it cannot harden them off. When I left the safe shelter of Kings Park School I was a very tender plant indeed, still shy with strangers and lacking self-confidence. For me, entering the Glasgow School of Art in October, 1946 was comparable to the Christian martyrs entering a den of lions.

It was not only the strange new routine that I found daunting. It was my fellow students. Those who were in my own age group were all right. I could feel on a par with them, for, like me, they were fresh from school and were learning the ropes. The ex-Service students, newly demobilised, were the unwitting cause of my unhappiness. In that year's intake, there were many of these mature students. No one grudged them their right to claim their long postponed places in college, but I think it would have been better had they been segregated from the school-leavers. Their maturity highlighted our own immaturity. It made me doubt my own capabilities. It made me feel that, in comparison with theirs, my own

talent was inadequate, at the very time when I needed encouragement to bolster my self-confidence. Some of these men had been
drawing and painting for years and had developed their own style
of work, a style that was as mature as they were themselves. I knew
two ex-Service students who had children older than I, so it was
literally a case of being at college with fellow students who were old
enough to be my father.

All the universities and colleges had made supreme efforts to
accept as many ex-Service students as possible in 1946 and, to
make room for them, the intake of school-leavers had to be
restricted. Those of us who were given places must have been
selected because we made the grade and that knowledge should
have been a comfort to us. Unfortunately, there was little comfort
in the further knowledge that too many students had been accepted
in October. The Director of Studies announced that the Board of
Governors had decided to reduce the number of students on the art
school roll, by means of an examination at Christmas. To pass
would mean continuation of studies. To fail would mean the end of
an art school road for that student. The pressure on us was so great
I could almost feel it, physically. The hothouse shelter of secondary
school was a thing of the past. I was being hardened off.

The fateful examination took place before Christmas and I
survived to return to art school in January 1947, for my second
term. Some, weeded out, did not return. My initial feeling of
strangeness had worn off completely and I found I had a proud
sense of belonging to my new seat of learning. Charities Day, in
that same month, saw me back on a lorry once more, dressed as a
dustman, (a topical theme at the time, for the city bin men were on
strike!), rattling my can and fleecing the citizens to the manner

born. I was coming out of my shell and beginning to enjoy my new life, at last.

The weather in January had been kind enough to us, that year, but it turned really nasty a few weeks later. Just when we might have expected spring to emerge, winter closed a tight grip upon us all. That proved to be the worst winter that I can remember, even to this day. Glasgow School of Art sits on top of a hill and, for weeks, the approaches to it were like sheet glass. We lost our footing regularly, not just once, but several times, on our way down the hill after classes each day. And so slippery was Renfrew Street that, like "the Grand Old Duke of York", when we were down, we were down! Getting up again, while holding an ungainly portfolio, was a job for more than one pair of hands. The picture that we presented would have been very comical, had it not become so monotonous. The bitter weather caused transport services to be disrupted and bus queues were long. This made us later than usual in arriving home after lectures. As we had to start out earlier than normal, to compensate for the road conditions, our college day was long.

The pressure was still on us to work hard for the sake of retaining our college places and there was always a lot of work to be completed at home. I grew accustomed to seeing the rest of my family going off to bed while I was still working at the table in the living room, painting or drawing or writing notes. I was seldom, if ever, in bed before one o'clock and often it was later than that. As long as I could keep warm, I did not mind the late hours of work. The crunch came when, in the depths of that dreadful cold spell, we ran out of coal at home. Completely. Literally. Totally. The cellar had been swept bare and not a burnable particle of fuel remained. Our coal merchant could not help us. He had no coal in his yard. I expect the snow and ice were to blame. The coal mines had been nationalised on 1st January that year, but any administrative teething troubles should have been overcome by the time of the big freeze in March/April. The shortage must have been due to the difficulty of moving coal in the prevailing weather conditions from the pits to the supply depots, I feel sure. No matter what the cause, the cold and bitter fact remained that we had no coal. I have the clearest recollection of sitting painting at the table in the small hours of the morning, sitting on my feet to keep them warm, dressed not in my overall, but in my overcoat!

Our family was not alone in its chilly plight. Many of our neighbours ran out of coal at that time, too. Frozen pipes were inevitable. Not only was there no water available in our house, there was none in the entire terrace block. We had to depend on the good nature and the good neighbourliness of an obliging householder, quite some way down our road. She still had water, and, for the duration of the big freeze-up, she put up with the daily inconvenience of having numerous buckets filled at her kitchen tap by processions of her less fortunate neighbours.

All this was happening in the "spring" of 1947, just one year after I had sat my Highers. In those comparatively early days of peacetime, I had looked to the future expecting to see an easing – or even a lifting – of the austerity that had marked our everyday lives since the beginning of the war. Yet here we all were, almost two years after the ending of the war, and austerity was not only still with us, it seemed to be biting even deeper into our peacetime lives than it had done in wartime. True, we no longer carried our gas masks. With joy, they had been consigned to the dustbin or condemned to perish in the attic, long ago. But we still carried our identity cards. We still had clothes rationing. And not only did we still have food rationing, but an additional commodity – bread and baker's sundries – had been put on coupons, as late as July, 1946! These special coupons were called "bread units" and were known as "B.U.s", for short.

Peacetime had turned out very differently from my childish conception of it. My daydreams of 6th June, 1944 truly had been "wishful thinking". The stark reality was beyond any dreams of mine. Time had shown me that war was not something to be snapped on and off again, like a light, leaving nothing changed. I could see now that war was like a severe injury, which left the patient weak, and from which recovery could be slow and barely perceptible for long periods. The time from the ending of the war until the ending of my first year as a full-time student at the Glasgow School of Art had been punctuated with events as horrible as any that we had heard of during the war. We had read of the spread of atomic bomb tests, at Bikini, condoned by governments and condemned by humanity. At Nuremberg, official trials of war criminals had gone on for months. From there, we had heard, but had not wanted to believe, the spine-chilling evidence of man's inhumanity to man.

I had entered my student days, shy and unsure of myself, still clinging to the last vestiges of my childhood. When I left, at the end of my first student year, I elected to go away, alone, to take a summer job in a strange place, where I did not know a soul. And, what is more, I looked forward to that, and to all the other new challenges that life – adult life – had to offer, not with trepidation but with anticipation, for the tender plant had been hardened off. I was no longer a child.

ACKNOWLEDGEMENTS

Mum typed her three originals in the 70s, on extremely thin A4 paper sandwiched between sheets of carbon paper, which she then fed into a very large, whirring IBM electric typewriter. (This was cutting edge technology, as far as we were concerned.) The completed copies were separated, compiled and then bound using a black plastic spine bar.

As she says in her Foreword, Mum wrote about her wartime childhood specifically for us. Our copies were handed over, accompanied by clear, oral instructions that we were not to share them with others, it being a very personal and private expression of her memories. It was, therefore, something of a surprise to us when, with us in our fifties and Mum in her eighties, Mum expressed a wish for us to bring a copy of her book to her. That "knowing look" Mum refers to in Chapter 12 was probably exchanged! After further investigation, it turned out that the questions about what it was like during the war had begun again, this time from interested and enthusiastic members of the Ballachulish care home staff. Commemorative programmes on various TV channels had prompted their initial interest, and where better to get more detailed information than from someone sitting right beside them.

From there, we finally get to here and a newly created copy of *Impressions of a Wartime Childhood* that looks like an actual, real-life book that can be shared with anyone Mum chooses to share it with. Once again her story can be shared across generations, with our additional hopes that no future generation of children will have to ask their mum the same questions we asked ours.

We very much wish to thank the following: the fantastic staff of Abbeyfield House, Ballachulish for their attentive care, especially to Paul and Bev for the stimulus; Maggie MacDonald for transposing Mum's words from the paper originals to more manageable computer file; and DJ for taking that computer file and "magically" transforming it into this!

Sarah & Helen, 2018

Printed in Poland
by Amazon Fulfillment
Poland Sp. z o.o., Wrocław

55321987R00094